The Life and Times of
CHARLES I

OVERLEAF LEFT Charles I at his trial, by
Edward Bower. Bower made sketches of the
King during the trial and then painted this
portrait of the King several times for
different patrons.
RIGHT An enamelled memorial locket with
a portrait of Charles I done on hair. It not
only bears the skull and crossbones, but
contains a piece of linen stained with blood,
supposedly the King's.

The Life and Times of
CHARLES I

D. R. Watson

Introduction by Antonia Fraser

Weidenfeld and Nicolson
London

Series design by Paul Watkins
Layout by Sasha Rowntree

Filmset by Keyspools Limited, Golborne, Lancashire
Printed and bound in Great Britain by
Butler & Tanner Ltd, Frome and London

Contents

Introduction

WHEN BERNINI looked at one of Van Dyck's great portraits of King Charles I, he pronounced it 'an unfortunate countenance'. Certainly of all our monarchs Charles, the sad-eyed Royal Martyr, can fairly claim to be the most ill-used: he alone, having been defeated by his subjects in battle, endured the extreme fate of death at their hands, after the pretence of a legal trial. Not only was his reign thus abruptly terminated but, his son and family fled, the Crown itself remained in abeyance for the next eleven years. It is, however, not so much the sufferings of King Charles I which make his story unique in our annals, although they lend much romantic pathos to the events of his life, it is rather the focus of these same sufferings – the English Civil War – which continues to be debated. And whichever way the argument goes, whether Charles is seen as the helpless puppet of social forces too vast to be contained by the strongest sovereign, or the narrow-minded bigot who by his thoughtless absolutism provoked the struggle, a consideration of his own personality is essential to determine the exact weight which should be given to it. Our most unfortunate King was at the same time England's most crucial ruler.

If Charles ended his life in drama and tragedy, he began it in an atmosphere of reserve and shyness. As the younger son of King James I, he was very much overshadowed by his glamorous elder brother the Prince of Wales, until his untimely death left Charles the heir. D. R. Watson's biography is particularly interesting in showing how much of the later sovereign had its roots in this hidden boyhood: we see how Charles's childhood gallantry in overcoming his physical handicaps, including a pronounced stammer, developed into the wretched obstinacy of the older man. Charles was nothing if not moral, 'blushing at an immodest word' unlike most of his close relations, including his father, or for that matter his son, the future Charles II; yet the loyal affection he was able to pour out unstintingly on a few individuals became concentrated on his Roman Catholic wife, the French Princess Henrietta Maria, to the credit of his private life, but with calamitous effects on his public policy. And one might add still further to his credit his wonderful patronage of the arts, even if aesthetic taste became expensive to a King who had not yet solved the problems of taxing his country efficiently.

The question remains: how far if at all did this private paragon justify the comment of Archbishop Laud that he knew neither how to be, nor how to be be made great? D. R. Watson, leading us with great skill and subtlety through the maze of contemporary argument and documentation, shows how central indeed to the complicated politics of the period was the peculiar character of the King. Charles was no revolutionary, grabbing new powers for the Crown, and he leant much on advice, seeing himself as shaping rather than creating new measures – a cobbler rather than a shoe-maker. But he had absolutely no sense of the limits of prudence, and in the vexed atmosphere of the 1630s was incapable of understanding that he might be legally right yet politically wrong. From 1640 on, all his most disquieting attributes came to the fore – his complete lack of insight and above all his inability to compromise, which he sought to conceal with a casuistry often seeming merely devious to outsiders. It was not until the end that his admirable personal qualities showed themselves again, and at the scene of the execution in 1649, once more 'He nothing common did or mean.' At the end of this clear and balanced narrative, we still retain our sympathy for Charles; yet it is only too easy to wonder, as Lucy Hutchinson reported at the time, how so good a man could prove so bad a King.

Antonia Fraser

Acknowledgments

Photographs and illustrations were supplied or are reproduced by kind permission of the following. The pictures on pages *2*, 16, *61*, 67, 68–9, 70, 72–3, 87, *125*, 190/1, 198–9, 202, *206*–7 are reproduced by gracious permission of H.M. the Queen; on page 78/1 by kind permission of the Duke of Devonshire; on page 62 by kind permission of the Duke of Portland; on page *64/2* by kind permission of the Earl of Pembroke; on page 94 by kind permission of Earl Fitzwilliam; on page 21 by kind permission of Baron Elibank; on page 194 by kind permission of Lord Primrose; on page 134/3 by kind permission of Lord Sackville; on pages 168 and 180/1 by kind permission of Lord Tollemache. Ashmolean Museum, Oxford: 134/2, 180/2; C.J. Bassham: 78/2; Birmingham City Museum and Art Gallery: 150; British Museum: 32–3, 40/1, 41, 76, 98–9, 109, 111, 118–9, 121, 122, 123/2, 144–5, 148/1, 149, 154, 171, 176–7, 190/3, 191, 196, 204/1, 211, 215; B.P.C.: 40/1, 52, 58, 109, 123/1, 171, 195; The Vicar, Church of St Chad: *128/2*; Bulloz: 116; Château de Versailles: 46–7; A.C. Cooper; *64/2*, 204/2; Courtauld Institute of Art: 79/1, 168; Cromwell House, Highgate: 148/2; Department of the Environment (Crown Copyright): 64/1, 158–9, 189/2; C.M. Dixon: *128/2*; Exeter Cathedral Library: 193; Fitzwilliam Museum, Cambridge: 14–5, 173; John Freeman: 32–3, 41, 80–1, 122, 126–7, 134/1, 154, 181, 188–9, 215; Giraudon: 46–7; House of Lords Record Office: 184–5; London Museum: 164–5; Louvre: 116; Mansell Collection: 40/3, 54, 55, 63, 174; Musées Royaux des Beaux Arts, Belgium: 52; National Army Museum: 133, 138–9; National Gallery: 203/1; National Maritime Museum: 77, 78/2; National Museum of Antiquities, Scotland: 3; National Portrait Gallery: 13, 28–29, *49*, 62, 85, 103, 110, *128/1*, 141, 192, 212; National Trust, Egremont Collection, Petworth: 167; Peter Jackson Collection: 181, 188–9; Public Record Office (Crown Copyright): 195; Radio Times Hulton Picture Library: 28–9, 37, 82, 84, 90, 92, 115, 146, 153, 160–1. 172; Rijksmuseum, Amsterdam: 106; Scottish National Portrait Gallery: 21, *194*; Society of Antiquaries: 10–11, 50–1; Trustees of the Grosvenor Estate: 203/2; Dr Van den Brent: 106; Victoria and Albert Museum: *113*, 135, 180/3, 190/1; Wayland Picture Library: 40/1; Derrick Witty: *64/1, 113*.

Picture research by Ann Mitchell.

The author and publishers would like to thank Christopher Hibbert for permission to quote from *Charles I* (Weidenfeld & Nicolson, 1968)

1 The Second Son 1600-23

THE CHILD who was to become King Charles I was born on 19 November 1600 in Dunfermline Castle, a few miles north of the Firth of Forth. His father was still King James VI of Scotland: another three years were to elapse before he succeeded Elizabeth on the English throne, and was able to move on a bigger stage, in a richer and more civilised country.

The baby Charles was the third child, and second son, of James and his Queen, Anne of Denmark. Their marriage had taken place in 1589, and the first child, Prince Henry, was born in 1594, followed by Elizabeth in 1596, and then by Charles four years later. The Queen had several other confinements, but all ended either in stillbirths or in the birth of weakly infants who did not survive the first few months of life. Charles was treated as very much the baby of the royal family, and was overshadowed by the accomplishments of his elder brother during the first twelve years of his life. Even when he was a young man his father's letters tended to refer to him still as 'Baby Charles'.

Charles was a sickly baby and was hurriedly baptised at birth as his life was almost despaired of. However, he survived the first four dangerous years, so often fatal at that time, even to the children of royalty who had every care and attention lavished upon them. Throughout this time he was in the care of Lord and Lady Fyvie at Dunfermline where the royal palace had a magnificent situation, close to the medieval abbey church, on a high bluff overlooking the rich farmland which stretched out southwards towards the broad waters of the Firth of Forth. In the distance the chimneys and rooftops of Edinburgh could be seen, perched on the narrow rocky ridge leading up to Edinburgh Castle. Queen Anne preferred Dunfermline to the capital, and spent much time there, while James tended to move around the different royal houses and hunting lodges, indulging his love of the chase.

In contrast to the vigorous first-born, their younger son gave the royal parents considerable cause for concern during his early years. He was very late to walk and to talk, having a weakness in the joints of his legs, and an impediment in his speech. He overcame the first of these defects and showed considerable physical stamina during the Civil War, though he remained of short stature. However, he never completely overcame the

PREVIOUS PAGES Prince Charles being welcomed home by his father, James I, in 1623, after the failure of his expedition to Spain to arrange a marriage with the Spanish Infanta.

OPPOSITE James I, a portrait by Daniel Mytens, painted in 1621 when the King was fifty-five.

The Thames at Richmond, with
the old Royal Palace in the
background; an early
seventeenth-century painting
by David Vinckeboons.

speech impediment, and this was, no doubt, one of the reasons for his shyness and reserve. His guardian reported to the Queen in 1604, when Charles was nearly four years old: 'Although yet weak in body, he is beginning to speak some words. He is far better as yet with his mind, than with his body and feet', and around the same time his doctor reported triumphantly that 'His Highness now walketh many times in a day all the length of the great chamber at Dunfermline like a gallant soldier all alone.' But there was probably some exaggeration in these claims. When Charles arrived in England his new guardian reported that he, 'was not able to go nor scant stand alone, he was so weak in his joints'.

When his father and mother left for England, along with his elder brother and sister, Charles had at first been left behind, as he had not appeared strong enough for the journey. He followed them south in August 1604, and was placed in the care of Sir Robert and Lady Cary, after several other noblemen's wives had refused the charge, fearing the responsibility of bringing up such a weak child. Lady Cary did her work well, and in view of the unhappy relationship between James and his Queen and the unpleasant atmosphere of the Jacobean Court, it was as well that custom demanded that royal children should spend their early years with what were virtually foster parents. One of Lady Cary's services to her young charge was preventing his father from ordering dangerous surgical meddling. Sir Robert Cary wrote in his memoirs:

> The King was desirous that the string under his tongue should be cut, for he was so long in beginning to speak as he thought he never would have spoke. Then he would have put him in iron boots, to strengthen his sinews and joints, but my wife protested so much against them both, as she got the victory, and the King was fain to yield. My wife had charge of him from a little past four till he was almost eleven years old, in all which time he grew more and more in health.

As a child, Charles, though said to be his mother's favourite, was very much in the shade of his elder brother, Henry, who possessed the physical strength and self-confidence that Charles so obviously lacked. Henry is said to have teased him 'till he made him weep, telling him that he should be a bishop, a gown being fittest to hide his legs'. On the whole, however, Charles

OPPOSITE Anne of Denmark, daughter of Frederick II of Denmark and Norway, Queen of James I and mother of Charles. The painting by Paul Van Somer shows her in hunting attire, with the palace of Oatlands in the distance.

does not seem to have resented his brother, but rather to have tried desperately to model himself on him. He was determined to become a skilful horseman, and in this, as in various other sports and manly exercises, he eventually succeeded. One of the appealing things about the character of Charles as a boy was this determination to overcome his handicaps and to acquire the accomplishments befitting a younger son of the King. In these early struggles developed the obstinacy which he was to show on many occasions in later life, in addition to the shyness and inner uncertainty that were to do him so much political harm.

Freudian psychology has convinced the modern world that 'the child is father to the man', and that the experiences of child-hood are decisive in moulding character. A biographer seeks information about the childhood of his subject which is rarely available in seventeenth-century sources. Even royal princes were not so closely observed that we can know much about their childhood. It was not until at least one hundred and fifty years later that people began to realise that children went through various stages of mental development. Young children were simply not paid a great deal of attention. So in seeking partially to explain Charles's personality by his early childhood we have to work from only a few hints and odd scraps of information. What we do know, however, fits into a plausible pattern. Charles in later life was shy and reserved, an introvert type, and a man who had great difficulty in ever seeing things from the point of view of others. On many occasions his language and actions were remarkably tactless. He was unsure of himself and tried very hard to hide his lack of self-confidence by a mask of royal dignity and authority. This often meant that he was obstinate on occasions when he should have given way. He had also a tendency to passivity. Time and again he took no action, when action was desperately needed. Much of this uncertainty can probably be accounted for by his physical endowment and the fact that during his first twelve years he was treated as the baby of the family. Charles, with his weak legs, speech impediment and general sense of inferiority, was completely dominated by the glamour of Henry, who was created Prince of Wales and endowed with a separate household while Charles was still a young boy.

Charles's education was grounded in the Latin language and

OPPOSITE Henry, Prince of Wales, on the hunting field with Robert Devereux, 3rd Earl of Essex, by Robert Peake the Elder. The precocious eldest son of James I, Henry's untimely death at the age of sixteen meant that his shy and retiring brother Charles became the heir to the throne.

the Christian religion. He never attained the scholarship of his father, and is reported to have been 'of as slow a pen as of speech', preferring to have his political speeches and declarations written by his advisers, but he had the usual intellectual equipment of a cultivated nobleman. The most important element in his education was the theological one and he remained, throughout his life, deeply religious and devoted to the Anglican Church. It has often been remarked that he was the first English monarch to have been brought up from childhood within the Church of England. Thus he was sympathetic to the 'High Church' doctrines that sought to establish the distinctive character of the Anglican creed, separated equally from Catholicism and from the extreme Protestant position. There can be no doubt that, for Elizabeth, the Church of England had been a political compromise. Her attitude contained no mystical element. James's theology was more complicated, but he did not have his son's devoutness. He had come to the Church of England late in life, whereas Charles was bred within its fold.

Charles's life was transformed in his twelfth year when his brother fell ill. The symptoms of Henry's disease first appeared in August 1612, and his condition grew rapidly worse. The preposterous treatment to which he was subjected, which included the application to his body of the flesh of newly killed cocks and pigeons, did not help, and by November his condition was desperate. The final treatment, a medicine concocted by Sir Walter Raleigh, consisting of pearl, musk, hartshorn, bezoarstone, mint, borage, gentian, mace, sugar, aloes and spirits of wine, administered on his mother's orders, together with a violent purge prescribed by the physician, was enough to kill him on 12 November 1612. He had probably been suffering from typhoid.

Charles was now the heir apparent, and at the age of twelve fulfilled his first official duty as chief mourner at his brother's funeral. The Queen was too grief-stricken to take part in the ceremony, and James did not attend, probably due to his morbid fear of disease and death. Charles's sister, the Princess Elizabeth, left for Germany shortly afterwards. Her marriage to a young German prince, Frederick the Elector Palatine, had been arranged for some time, and had been postponed because of her brother's illness and death. The Queen, left alone with her

OPPOSITE Charles I as Duke of York, by Robert Peake the Elder, c. 1610.

21

younger son, attempted to take charge of his education, but James forbade her to interfere. Anne was not an intelligent woman, and her chief interests were jewels, fine clothes, masques and dances. Charles, a serious minded child, had already gone beyond his mother's intellectual reach.

Shortly after Henry's death, James began to make plans for his new heir's marriage. This was, of course, to be part of a diplomatic arrangement. Although ten years were to pass before Charles's marriage actually took place, the question was prominent in James's foreign policy for the rest of his reign. He considered first an alliance with the French royal House, but soon turned towards Spain. In 1604, as soon as he came to the English throne, James had put an end to the old war with Spain. This was a sensible policy. Warfare offered rare and rich prizes to a few, but at the cost of far greater losses to the majority, caused by the disruption of normal economic life. James had followed up this peace treaty by playing an important role as mediator between the Spanish and the Dutch in the negotiations leading to the treaty of 1609, which ended the long drawn out war after the Dutch revolt against Spanish rule.

For the next few years James saw himself as the European peacemaker, holding the balance between the Protestant and Catholic powers and bringing about a general European settlement. This vision was not altogether unrealistic. England was only a small power compared to the giant military monarchies of France, Spain and the Habsburg Empire, but by balancing between the different parties, she could play a role greater than that really warranted by her strength, and thus improve her own material interests as well as the prestige of her royal House. It would be a fine stroke for James, only recently the impoverished King of a tiny and remote kingdom, to marry his son to the Spanish Infanta, daughter of the leading royal House of Europe. James had arranged the marriage of his daughter Elizabeth to the Elector Palatine, one of the leading Protestant princes of Germany, as part of his scheme. Charles's marriage to the Spanish Infanta would counterbalance the other marriage and demonstrate that England was committed to neither the extreme Protestant nor the militant Catholic party.

In fact James's scheme was a good deal too grandiose. At the very least, the Spanish demands were such that they would, if accepted, have provided the possibility of turning England into a Spanish satellite. In the long run they were aiming at nothing less than the reimposition of Catholicism as the national religion. James's policy did a great deal of harm to the royal position in England because of these domestic and religious implications. There was too much anti-Spanish and anti-Catholic feeling in England for the marriage of the royal heir to a Spanish princess to be regarded with equanimity. Peace with Spain was one thing; a Spanish Queen quite another. Moreover the hope that the Protestant–Catholic conflict in Europe was drawing to a close was rudely shattered by the outbreak of the Thirty Years' War in 1618.

James was involved in this conflict, for it was precipitated by his son-in-law, the Elector Palatine's decision to accept the crown of Bohemia, thereby placing himself at the head of Protestant Czech rebels who were challenging the Habsburg power at a crucial point. The result was to be disastrous for Frederick personally and for the peace of Germany and Europe. The Czechs were defeated at the battle of the White Mountain, and Frederick soon lost not only Bohemia, but also most of his original possessions in the Palatinate. For many years the desire to re-establish Frederick and his English bride, the Princess Elizabeth, to their original state, remained an element in the policy of James, and later of Charles. At first James refused to admit that this involved a breach with Spain. He hoped that the terms of Charles's proposed marriage to the Spanish Infanta would include Spanish pressure on their Habsburg cousins to restore Frederick to his former position in the Palatinate. This was not a real possibility, but was dangled before him for some time by the Spaniards and allowed the negotiations to continue.

Charles was too young to take a personal interest in his father's diplomacy for most of this period. For him the most important development of these years was his close relationship with his father's favourite, George Villiers, successively created knight, Viscount, Earl, Marquis, and finally Duke of Buckingham. Originally the penniless younger son of a minor noble family, he and his clan gradually monopolised royal favours. Among all the political factors leading to the fall of the Stuart monarchy, James's and Charles's infatuation for this beautiful young man was vital. Villiers exemplified all that was worst in the system of

Court patronage and influence. Moreover he was hopelessly incompetent, and his policies concerning both home and foreign affairs were uniformly unsuccessful. From 1618 Villiers dominated James, and presided over the deterioration of relations between the Crown and the majority of the gentry represented in Parliament. This deterioration was to lead, like a long-delayed fuse, to the final explosion that destroyed Charles. The stage was set for the conflict between Crown and Parliament during the period from 1621 to 1628, when Villiers ruled, first through his influence over James, and then over Charles.

When the young Villiers first became his father's favourite Charles is said to have been jealous and hostile towards him. But Villiers, knowing well his long-term interest, was determined to win over the young prince and directed as much charm on him as on his father. James used his paternal influence, insisting on a formal reconciliation between the Prince of Wales (the title conferred on Charles in November 1616) and Villiers. A sumptuous banquet marked the occasion in June 1618. At this feast James went over to Villiers's relatives and swore that he and his descendants 'would advance that House above all others whatsoever'. After this breaking of the ice Charles became attached to Villiers, who soon became his close companion. The elegant, accomplished, and superficially clever young man came to occupy the role previously played in Charles's life by his elder brother Henry. At this stage in life, lacking confidence in himself, Charles had need of a slightly older man, to whom he could turn for advice and as an example. His father was hardly an appropriate model, and it seems that Charles's abstemiousness, his exquisite manners and rigorous sexual morality were a tacit condemnation of his father. But all outward respect was shown to the King, and Charles probably also had a good deal of affection for his father. Some of this appears in the letters written jointly with Villiers to James from Spain in 1623. However, the grotesque nature of James's habits and his complete lack of reserve when his affections were engaged, were in marked contrast to the delicacy of Charles's manners and his physical self-control.

The Queen died on 2 March 1619. Once again, as during his eldest son's illness, James avoided the deathbed. Charles was present and sought to comfort his mother during her last illness.

Queen of Bohemia.

Elizabeth, daughter of James I, by G. Honthorst. She married Frederick, the Elector Palatine in 1613. Charles never saw her again, but his foreign policy was dominated by attempts to help her and her husband regain their lands in the Palatinate and Bohemia, lost at the outset of the Thirty Years' War.

By now he had overcome the physical defects of his childhood and, though short, was a dignified and accomplished young man. The Venetian ambassador reported in 1621: 'He was dignified in manner and active in habits. He rode well and distinguished himself at tennis and at the tilting yard. He had good taste in music and painting. His moral conduct was irreproachable and he used to blush at an immodest word.'

From this time Charles began to play a role in politics. His first political act was during the Parliament of 1621, when he was sent to plead for Francis Bacon before the House of Lords where he was being impeached, one of several victims of Parliamentary wrath. This Parliament typified the early stages of the conflict with the Stuart monarchy that was to bring Charles to his death. It had been called because of dangerous developments on the international scene. James's desire to see a general reconciliation between Catholics and Protestants in Europe had been struck a devasting blow by the outbreak of the Thirty Years' War in Germany. His own son-in-law was largely responsible. By placing himself at the head of the Czech rebels, he had not only failed to win himself a kingdom in Bohemia, but had lost his original territory, the Palatinate, along the Rhine. The Habsburg family was acting in concert once again: Spain seized the opportunity to strengthen her position in Northern Europe, invading Frederick's territory from the Spanish Netherlands; meanwhile the Austrian branch of the family chased him and his troops from the field of the White Mountain, ending Czech independence for three centuries. James did not support Frederick's ambitious plans for the Bohemian Crown, but could scarcely stand by and watch his daughter and son-in-law being turned into landless fugitives without making some protest. He hoped at least to save their land in the Palatinate, preferably by agreement with Spain. But even if negotiation was his aim it was essential to show that military support might be given. In order for England to offer any sort of military credibility, it was necessary to call a Parliament to raise money.

The calling of Parliament in 1621 was to prove a bitter disappointment to James. Instead of voting supplies it embarked upon an examination of grievances that was to go far. Resentment against the Buckingham clan was a principal reason for this opposition. Sir Edward Coke, at one time Lord Chief Justice, who had been dismissed from office in 1616 because of a collision with James over the interpretation of the law regarding the extent of prerogative power, was one of Buckingham's enemies. He now turned his formidable intellectual powers and legal erudition to the task of using ancient precedent and medieval legal forms to challenge royal power through Parliament. His most ingenious device was the revival of the medieval form of impeachment as a way of removing unpopular royal favourites. There had been no cases of impeachment between 1459 and 1621; under the Tudors, Acts of Attainder had been used to remove defeated statesmen. But an Act of

Attainder required the royal assent. Impeachment was a form of judicial procedure in which Parliament acted as a court, with the Commons prosecuting and the Lords judging; the King was not involved. At this point the great favourite himself was spared, but his creatures were not. Both Giles Mompesson, the most notorious monopolist, and Francis Bacon, who had succeeded Coke as Chief Justice, and had been much more favourable towards royal claims, were impeached.

The House of Commons gave limited financial aid, voting only two subsidies, and insisted on debating foreign policy despite James's protest that such questions were his alone to decide. This produced as a reply from the Commons the Protestation of 18 December 1621, in which were asserted the privileges of Parliament, 'the ancient and undoubted inheritance of the subjects of England', including the right to free speech in Parliament. The King dissolved Parliament and tore the record of the Protestation out of the Commons Journals with his own hands.

All hope of threatening war to defend the Elector Palatine now abandoned, James returned with even greater assiduity to his plan to marry Charles to the Spanish Infanta, hoping to halt Spain's aggressive policy in Germany as part of the marriage settlement. This diplomacy remained unsuccessful, and the affair's main interest here lies in Charles's romantic escapade of an *incognito* visit to Madrid in the company of Buckingham. James for a long time resisted the idea, but eventually gave way to the insistence of the two young men. However it is hard to imagine that he can really have expected their personal diplomacy to achieve very much.

On 18 February 1623 two young men calling themselves Jack and Tom Smith crossed the river at Gravesend by ferry. Wearing obviously false beards, everything they did seemed designed to arouse suspicion. They overpaid the ferryman, and asked him to put them ashore outside Gravesend, instead of at the usual landing place. On meeting a royal coach on the Dover road, they turned away and crossed the fields. A messenger sent back by the coach's escort gave the alert and they were arrested on their arrival at Canterbury. On being brought before the Mayor, Tom Smith revealed himself to be the Marquis of Buckingham and declared that he was on his way secretly to inspect the fleet, being Lord Admiral among his

'Sweet boys and dear venturous knights'

27

The ceremonial entry of
Prince Charles and the
Duke of Buckingham into
Madrid in March 1623.
Their impetuous
expedition to Spain to woo
the Spanish Infanta in
person greatly embarrassed
the Spanish King and
embittered relations
between England
and Spain.

29

many offices. They were allowed to proceed and crossed the Channel, but the secret was out. By the time Paris was reached everyone at Court knew that they were off to Madrid to woo the Spanish princess. They halted for two days in Paris and managed, as touring gentlemen, to obtain permission to visit the Court and see a masque, in which the young Henrietta Maria, soon to be Charles's bride, was performing. They then rode on, keeping up a good pace, and reached Madrid on 7 March.

Charles could not be officially presented at Court as he was travelling *incognito* and without a suitable suite, but arrangements were made for the Infanta and her suitor to see each other. Charles and Buckingham sat in a coach while the Spanish Royal Family drove up and down the street. A remarkable feature of this affair is that Charles seems to have convinced himself that he really was in love, although he had only brief and formal conversations with the Infanta. On one occasion he jumped over a wall into a garden where the Infanta was walking with some of the Court ladies; she fled in confusion. In reality, for all Charles's play-acting in the style of Renaissance 'preciosity', there could be no question of sweeping the Infanta off her feet with declarations of passionate love. That style served Buckingham well in his flirtations with the wives and daughters of the Spanish nobility, but Charles's marriage was a matter of high policy and involved hard diplomatic bargaining.

The Spanish King was highly embarrassed, in fact, by Charles's arrival and had no intention of committing himself to the marriage. The first excuse was that a papal dispensation would have to be obtained to allow the Infanta to marry a heretic. An envoy was despatched to Rome to ask the Pope for this dispensation, with another hard at his heels to ask him confidentially not to grant it. However, the Pope refused to play the Spanish game, hoping that the marriage would lead to the easing of life for English Catholics. The dispensation was granted, but under rigorous conditions. This forced the Spaniards to make yet further conditions, hoping to dissuade the importunate suitor. It took Charles a long time to realise that whenever he conceded one point, another, even more difficult for him to implement, would be demanded. Finally the Spanish King demanded that the marriage be preceded by a year's betrothal in order to test English good faith; if, at the end of that period, the promised concessions to English Catholics had been made, the marriage would take place. This was Philip's final effort to impose impossible terms, but Charles accepted even this humiliation, and the 'betrothal' was celebrated with due pomp. But it appears that his agreement was feigned. Charles had been infected by the crazy fears of his father, whose anxious letters to his two boys had pursued them to Madrid at frequent intervals. Among these was the notion that the Spaniards would hold Charles hostage if the marriage were not arranged; this was a ludicrous misreading of Spanish intentions. In order to avoid this imaginary danger, Charles agreed to all the Spanish conditions and then set off for England, by ship, from the north-west coast of Spain. On leaving Spanish soil he repudiated his signature, and when he and Buckingham returned to England they were as eager for the declaration of war on Spain as they had previously been for a Spanish marriage. They landed at Portsmouth on 5 October, amid general rejoicing that the heir to the throne had returned safe and sound, unmarried and a Protestant, for there had even been scare rumours of his conversion to Catholicism.

It was time for their return, for James, though only fifty-seven, was almost senile and it was probable that he would not live long. He was steadily becoming less capable of taking the decisions necessary for the functioning of the government. The control of British policy really lay with Buckingham, from his return from Spain in October 1623 to the time of his assassination in 1628, thanks to his ascendancy over both James and Charles. The death of James in March 1625 was little more than an incident which scarcely disturbed the political situation. For a short time after his accession it seemed that Charles would be able to capitalise on the benefits of being a new ruler and a much more attractive figure than the old King. But the continuance of old policies and the dominance of Buckingham meant that this potential advantage was thrown away: within a very short time all the old quarrels were renewed with increased bitterness.

'I care for match nor nothing, so I once have you in my arms again'

a Confectioner a S

a Sadler a Porter

a Glover a Meal- m

2 The Royal Inheritance 1624-7

a Box-maker

a Sope-boyler

a Taylor

a Chick   en-man

a Button- maker

a Sho=maker

How should we seek to describe the three kingdoms of which Charles became ruler when his father died in March 1625? In the first place they contained many fewer people than the same area today. We do not have exact statistics, but the population of the British Isles at that time was less than one tenth of the present population, certainly less than five million. To our eyes it would seem above all a rural and agricultural population. Only London would be big enough to rate as a city today, and London overshadowed all other towns with a population of perhaps 250,000, while Bristol, Norwich and York had around 10,000. No other town had more than a few thousand inhabitants. But regarded in contemporary terms, most of England at least, if not Wales, Ireland and Scotland, was relatively densely populated. Forest and wasteland were rare, and most of the land area was tilled and inhabited. England was a small country, where nature had been tamed, while in the rest of Western Europe there remained vast tracts of semi-wilderness. Further eastwards in Europe, settled areas became increasingly mere isolated clearings in the surrounding forest and waste. The Celtic fringe of the British Isles shared some of these characteristics, but the south and east and the Midlands of England were peaceful and well populated.

This relatively dense population meant that roads and bridges, however inadequate in our eyes, were better than in many other parts of Europe. Communications were good in England, and this was one reason, in addition to the fact that an island was protected from foreign invasion, for the unique political developments here. By the beginning of the seventeenth century England was more of a political unit, ruled centrally from London, than any other European state. The great monarchies of France and Spain, albeit impressive on a map, were in many ways only loose federations of provinces and local communities, which retained much of their local independence. The immense empire of the Habsburgs shared these characteristics to an even greater degree. From the early Middle Ages royal justice and taxation had been centred on London in a way that differed from the other kingdoms of Europe. Out of this had grown the unique institution of the English Parliament, a body in many ways unlike the various representative assemblies of the Continent. This political centralisation applied only to

PREVIOUS PAGES London tradesmen in 1647. By the middle of the seventeenth century one Englishman in fourteen was a Londoner and no town in England was one tenth as populous as the capital.

34

England. One of Charles's mistakes was to think that he could act as though it extended to Scotland and Ireland as well. From reactions to his policies in these outlying regions sprang the great crisis of the Civil War that brought him to his death.

The people ruled by Charles were, by our standards, undoubtedly extremely poor. A few aristocrats had immense wealth, a small group of merchants and landowners were reasonably prosperous, but the great majority of the population lived in terrible poverty. Again, however, it is as well to make comparisons with other areas of Europe at that time. Though exact statistics are lacking, there can be little doubt that the standard of living of the ordinary rural population in England was higher than that of most other parts of Europe. The most telling evidence is provided by demographers who have studied fluctuations in the death rate. Whereas, in many parts of Europe, the seventeenth century saw recurrent periods of demographic crisis, two or three years in which the population fell dramatically due to enormous mortality, it seems clear that such crises were absent in England. The explanation is that in England the pressure of the population on the food supply was not so acute. In Europe a bad harvest, or two or three consecutive bad harvests, produced famine conditions with resultant starvation, despite all government efforts to control the price of grain. The population, weakened by malnutrition, fell prey to disease, and epidemics of infectious maladies, bubonic plague and other less well defined diseases, made the situation worse. Although a bad harvest in England produced a time of hardship and dearth, especially when, as in 1648, the situation was worsened by warfare, it did not produce an absolute catastrophe like those across the Channel. The inference is that the margin of safety was rather greater in England. English society in the early seventeenth century had already achieved a general level of well-being reached only in the mid-eighteenth century by most of Western Europe.

A comparison between England and the Continent also highlights the extent to which commerce and industry had already developed in England by the seventeenth century. A rural society by present-day standards, England was nevertheless already sowing the seeds of the eighteenth-century industrial revolution. A wholly agricultural society would not have been

The Era of Witch-hunts

It was during the seventeenth century that the majority of witchcraft accusations in England took place. Witchcraft was an ecclesiastical offence in the Middle Ages and only became a civil offence by Act of Parliament in 1542. The law was made more severe in 1604 and was not repealed until 1736. The main offences were injuring people or property, causing human death and conjuring evil spirits, and death was the punishment for these offences from 1604 onwards.

Witches Apprehended, Ex·
amined and Executed, for notable
villanies by them committed both by
Land and Water.

With a strange and most true triall how to know
whether a woman be a Witch
or not.

Printed at London for *Edward Marchant*, and are to be sold at his shop ouer against the Crosse in Pauls Church-yard. 1 6 1 3.

LEFT The title-page of a book on witchcraft, with an account of a witch's trial. Unlike Scotland or the Continent, suspected witches in England were not usually tortured, and death was by hanging, not burning.

RIGHT Matthew Hopkins, notorious witch-hunter during the Civil War. Between 1645 and 1647 he and John Stearn toured the eastern counties and rounded up several hundred suspected witches.

so disturbed by the economic depression, centred on the woollen trades, that hit England at the end of James's reign. It has also been pointed out that Charles's period of non-Parliamentary government in the 1630s was dependent on the existence of commercial and capitalistic elements in the social structure of Stuart England that allowed Charles to defy the landowning classes represented in Parliament. It has been said that had England possessed a purely agricultural economy the Crown might have become the puppet of the landowning class. This happened, for instance, in Poland, and, for some periods of the eighteenth century, in Sweden. The balance between agriculture, commerce and industry was more finely set in England, and this economic complexity made possible a more complex political system.

The other striking feature of English society, in contrast with that of the Continent, was the absence of a rigid dividing line between nobility and commoners. There was an English nobility, of course, but it was tiny. Even after James's creations there were only 122 English peers and less than two thousand knights. The knights themselves were not distinguished from commoners by legal privileges like those separating the nobility from the common people in nearly every Continental state. This was a basic fact of English social and political history of immense significance in the evolution of Parliament into an effective political force. Continental representative assemblies were divided into separate 'estates'; details varied from state to state, but there were normally three, the clergy, the nobility and the commoners. This reflected the fact that on the Continent the nobility comprised a sizeable proportion of the population, which varied according to area, but was numbered in tens or hundreds of thousands against the 122 English peers. The English gentry were equivalent to the noble estate on the Continent; some of them had the title of knight, some merely 'esquire', and some used no title at all. There were informal social distinctions in England and some formal ones, such as the right, obtained from the College of Heralds, to bear a coat of arms. But these distinctions were trivial in comparison with the solid legal, fiscal and political privileges marking off the noble estate on the Continent. Thus there was a fundamental difference between the English Parliament and the Continental estates.

Another point of contrast lay in the possession by most Western European monarchs of a large body of civilian officials and an army: the English king had neither. Local administration, including the collection of taxes and the dispensing of justice in minor cases, was handled by the local gentry, acting unpaid as justices of the peace, either individually or meeting together at quarter-sessions to deal with the more general and more important questions. Although customs such as the purchase and inheritance of office meant that royal bureaucracies on the Continent were considerably more independent of the monarch than might appear at first sight, there was still a great difference between the administrative systems of the great Continental monarchies and the English system of self government by the landed gentry. In addition, the fact that the English king had no permanent military force of any size on which to call, emphasises how very different was his situation from that of his European royal cousins. It was not so much that his power was less than theirs. They could be challenged and frequently were by rebellious oppositions. But that was usually the result of some localised revolt, in a particular area or province, and would take the form of armed resistance. Charles, it is true, eventually managed to produce armed conflict in England, but it was unusual here, while endemic on the Continent, and certainly did not constitute the rebellion of an outlying province against the centre. Rather, in 1642, it was the King who was forced into the periphery, while Parliament retained a firm hold on political and economic power at the centre.

Relations between the monarch and the politically important class, the landowning gentry, had developed under the Tudors in a way unique in Europe, in the form of the Parliamentary system worked so well by Elizabeth. This was an important factor in allowing England to escape, for the most part, the religious wars between Catholics and Protestants that had devastated so much of Europe in the sixteenth century. Another element in Elizabeth's success was her achievement of a theological compromise in the Anglican Church, whose doctrines were sufficiently broad and ill defined to include widely divergent tendencies. Just how far apart these tendencies could become was only to be revealed during and after the Civil War, but there can be no doubt that their origins lay in the period of

Town and Country

England in the seventeenth century was still a rural society by present-day standards, although the seeds of the eighteenth-century industrial society were being sown. In the reign of Charles I there were perhaps 8000 knights and esquires, and more than 10,000 lower gentry. It was in the country that these gentlemen normally lived out their lives, though London society was beginning to attract the wealthier among them.

ABOVE A countrywoman on her way to market.
FAR LEFT A countrywoman carrying a shopping basket, from Hollar's *Ornatus Mulierbris*. Her shoes are raised on pattens to protect her from the filth of the roads.
LEFT An etching by Hollar showing a fashionable lady attired for winter. She wears a loo-mask, and carries a muff and stole.

RIGHT Robert Vaughan's engraving of 'The English Gentleman' in 1630. The surrounding scenes show different aspects of his prosperous and well-ordered life.

YOVTH

RECREATION

Non arcum semper tendit Apollo

The English Gentleman

SPES IN CÆLIS

Virtute tuá.

Vox lata sed anxia letii.

DISPOSITION.

ACQVAINTANCE

Certus amor morum est

EDVCATION

Vbera et verbera

123
1619

MODERATION

Moderata durant

VOCATION

PES IN TERRIS.

PERFECTION

Generoso Germine Gemma.

sixteenth-century Reformation. A potentially dangerous conflict, between the extreme Puritan elements and those whose quarrel with the 'bishop of Rome' had not been pressed to such lengths, was already present under Elizabeth. At a time when political conflicts very often found expression in theological terms, and when the organisation of the Church was seen by everyone as a vital part of the social and political structure, the Elizabethan compromise over religion was an essential element in the preservation of national unity and domestic political peace. The two instruments handed over by Elizabeth to her Stuart successors with which to rule their new country were the Church of England and Parliament, managed by skilful policy and careful patronage, so as to co-operate with the Crown, and not to challenge it. The breakdown of the Elizabethan compromise under James I and Charles I proceeded by parallel steps in the Church and in Parliament, linking together theological conflict and questions of taxation and foreign policy.

The last year of James's reign, and the first three years of that of his son, were to see England engaged in war. This was the only period between 1604 and 1650 in which foreign warfare took place. There were no very good reasons for this bellicosity which must mainly be attributed to Buckingham's temperament. To him war was indeed the sport of kings. The cavalier way in which he swung from the Spanish marriage to war against Spain, and equally rapidly from a French marriage actually concluded, to war against France, demonstrated the amazing extent to which serious questions of policy were judged as trivial personal quarrels.

Immediately upon their return from Spain, Charles and Buckingham pressed for the declaration of war on that country. This necessitated the calling of Parliament to vote money. The last Parliament of James's reign assembled in February 1624, and enthusiastically voted for war with Spain. Lords and Commons assembled in the great hall at Whitehall Palace to hear Buckingham and Charles report on their Spanish journey. Buckingham gave a very biased account of the negotiations, turning at intervals to Charles who nodded agreement. James was very reluctant to endorse this change in policy and even more reluctant to appear to do so at the behest of Parliament. It was precisely Parliament's claim to debate foreign policy that had led him, in 1621, to tear the pages out of the Commons' Journals. Buckingham, thinking he could ride the wave of popular anti-Spanish feeling, made many concessions to Parliament, even allowing the impeachment of the Lord Treasurer, Lionel Cranfield, Earl of Middlesex, a financial expert who had risen with Buckingham and provided such efficiency as there had been in the government during these years. James had turned to Buckingham and said with considerable prescience, 'You are making a rod with which you will be scourged yourself.' He is also supposed to have told Charles, 'You will live to have your bellyful of parliaments.'

'You will live to have your bellyful of parliaments

Parliament voted an inadequate sum of money and stated in the preamble to the subsidy bill that it should only be used for the defence of the kingdom, for the navy, for Ireland, or to aid the Dutch. They advocated a naval war against Spain and forbade the Continental expedition planned by Charles and Buckingham to recover the Palatinate for Frederick. As part of this policy the latter made a treaty with France, soon to be cemented by Charles's marriage to Henrietta Maria, the young princess, sister to King Louis XIII. The terms of this marriage agreement included a promise by Charles to give English Catholics all the concessions previously promised to Spain. At the same time he was telling Parliament that he would follow a vigorous policy of persecution. Already that duplicity was evident which was to harm him so much politically.

The negotiations with France, governed by Cardinal Richelieu, went ahead more rapidly than those with Spain and were scarcely delayed by James's death. In May 1625 agreement was reached and a marriage ceremony took place, by proxy, at Notre Dame Cathedral in Paris. The fourteen-year-old Henrietta Maria, still a child physically and emotionally, set off to cross the Channel from Boulogne to Dover a little over a month later. Charles, playing the romantic lover again, watched for her ship from the roof of Dover Castle. When they met for the first time on the morning after her landing her immaturity was apparent. After their first embrace she began to make the formal speech she had been taught, but through nervousness forgot her words and burst into tears. Charles sought to comfort her, saying 'She was not fallen into the hands of enemies and strangers, but into the wise disposal of God, who would have her leave her kindred and cleave to her spouse.' Very conscious of her small stature, she thought that Charles was glancing down to see if she were wearing high-heeled shoes; she swept aside her skirts to show him her shoes, saying: 'Sire, I stand on mine own two feet: I have no helps by art; thus high am I, neither higher nor lower.'

On 12 June 1625 another marriage ceremony took place at Canterbury. That night, after a marriage banquet, Charles and Henrietta Maria were alone together for the first time. Next morning it was reported that Charles was 'jocund' but Henrietta Maria 'very melancholy'. Four years later their marriage was to blossom into a romantic idyll, but at first things did not go well. Henrietta Maria was only a child, and Charles, who as a royal prince at his father's Court had remained remarkably untouched by the surrounding atmosphere, is reliably reported to have had no sexual experience before marriage. In any case the difficulties they encountered were not only physical. The Queen was too young to adjust easily to a new life in a foreign country. She remained surrounded by her French attendants, who did nothing to smooth the adjustment, behaving arrogantly and quarrelling with other members of the Court. Charles eventually decided to take the bull by the horns and sent all her train back to France in defiance of the terms of the marriage treaty. This was in August 1626, and by this time the personal relationship of Charles and Henrietta Maria had become thoroughly entangled in political matters.

Buckingham had from the first done all he could to worsen relations between the King and his bride, for he wanted no rival to deprive him of his monopoly of royal power. Charles recounted his quarrels with the Queen in detail to Buckingham. These culminated in an occasion in July 1626 when Charles told her that he would not allow her to appoint French courtiers as her household officers. Charles wrote to Buckingham:

> Then she said, all those in the paper [a list of names which she had handed to Charles] had brevates from her mother and herself, and she could admit no other. Then I said it was neither in her mother's power nor hers to admit any without my leave: and that, if she stood upon that, whomsoever she recommended should not come in. Then she bade me plainly take my lands to myself: for, if she

44

had no power to put in whom she would in these places, she would have neither lands nor houses of me: but bade me give her what I thought fit in pension. I bade her then remember to whom she spoke: and told her that she ought not to use me so. Then she fell into a passionate discourse, how miserable she was in having no power to place servants, and that business succeeded the worse for her recommendations which, when I offered to answer she would not so much as hear me. Then she went on, saying she was not of that base quality to be used so ill. Then I made her both hear me and end that discourse.

After this Charles determined to send away all her servants and did so, despite the poor girl's desperate protests. He is said to have dragged her by force away from the window at which she was trying to speak to her departing servants. Charles wrote to Buckingham on 7 August 1626: 'I command you send all the French away tomorrow out of the town. If you can, by fair means (but stick not long in disputing) otherwise force them away, driving them away like so many wild beasts, until you have shifted them; and so the devil go with them.'

'I command you send all the French away tomorrow out of the town'

This insult could well have been made the occasion of a breach between the two countries, but Richelieu was determined to remain on good terms with England if possible. Tactful reproaches forced Charles to allow his Queen to have a new and smaller French entourage. But Buckingham, whose inconsequential policy was now reaching lunatic levels, did not let this deter him. He forced a war with France, while remaining at war with Spain; in the latter case offensive operations had virtually ceased, after the fiasco of an attack on Cadiz, and the total eclipse of an English expedition to the Low Countries under the command of the German *condottiere* Mansfeld. This expedition had been so mismanaged that the unfortunate troops, pressed unwillingly into service, nearly all died of disease and inadequate food while awaiting permission to land, first in France, then in Holland.

The marriage settlement had shown the total diplomatic incompetence of Buckingham: aimed at building a great alliance against Spain to recover the Palatinate for Frederick, that perpetual mirage of Stuart policy, the marriage had been concluded with only vague promises on the French side. In return England had undertaken to make concessions to her Catholic subjects

45

The French successfully landing on the Ile de Ré in November 1627. The English expedition, led by Buckingham, which had been sent to relieve the Protestant citizens of La Rochelle, landed on the nearby Ile de Ré and soon retreated in disorder in the face of the French.

OPPOSITE George Villiers, Duke of Buckingham, by an unknown artist. The handsome favourite of two kings, he wielded immense power to disastrous effect. He was the last royal favourite to have real political power.

and to lend ships which the French could use against their Protestant rebels. Both these promises were abandoned in the face of Parliamentary opposition, but, hoping to make the best of a bad job, the French were conciliatory. Richelieu had the chagrin of realising that diplomatic finesse was of little avail in dealing with a clumsy braggart like Buckingham; the English simply ignored the advantageous terms of the marriage treaty. Even then it was not Richelieu but Buckingham who insisted on a quarrel; thrusting himself into internal French politics, he sailed in 1627 to the relief of the Protestant city of La Rochelle, before its citizens had finally broken with the French king or asked for help. When Buckingham arrived they were persuaded to do so, disastrously for them. He encamped on the Ile de Ré and was helped by the citizens of La Rochelle rather than the other way round. Soon the English were driven ignominiously home and La Rochelle fell to the French King, the beginning of the end of the privileged position held by the Huguenots in France.

George Villers
Duke of Bukingham.

Greate Brittaines Noble and worth

To the right Hon
Oliver Viscount Grandison
George Lo: Carew
Fulke Lo: Brooke
Arthur Lo: Chichester
Sr Edward Conway
Sr Horace Vere
Sr Edward Cecill
Sr Robert Mansell
Sr Iohn Oagle
Sr Thomas Button
Yo.r Ho.nors humble servant

Printed for Thomas Archer, in Popes head Alley, and are to be sold at his shop in Popes head Alley, over against the signe of the Horse-shoe.

The God of Warre lookes donne, and from his eies
Shoots smiles of ioy to see what Pollicies
Are read (here) in this Schoole: This Councell-Boord
(Vpheld by tenne braue Souldiers) does afford

Matter (by Armes) to heighten Englands State,
These bem more great then Romes Decemuirate
Happiest of Kings is ours: who in his Throne
Sits, Kissing Peace, enioying her alone:

More then all Christian
Beate at his Neighbours
This heape of Worthies; an
How to guard Strangers

ouncell of WARR

e) yt when Drums Th Souldier fights abroad, but these at home
s, forthwith comes Teach him to fight well: From these ten Heads come
is knowne. Those streames of Councell, by which War does stand
auide our owne. As far. as in the Ocean does this Land.

3 Unruly Parliaments 1625-9

Not only foreign affairs went badly in these years. Warfare meant calling Parliament to ask for financial support. But in spite of the fact that Buckingham throughout assumed that his foreign policy of war against Catholic Spain and France would be popular, Parliament proved very reluctant to vote the necessary money. Instead it turned its attention to protests against the favourite and against the expedients to which the government resorted in an attempt to make up for the money that was not voted. A vicious circle set in, in which relations between Charles and his Parliaments went from bad to worse. He was never really to overcome the effects of the three disastrous years under Buckingham's tutelage.

The 1625 Parliament met first in London, then in Oxford to avoid the plague raging in the capital. The King and Buckingham made no serious attempt to explain their policy, a line of action in which they were no doubt justified in strictly legal terms. But it was unwise political tactics, and the capital of goodwill which might have benefited the new reign was at once dissipated. The Oxford Parliament voted only two subsidies, a sum wholly inadequate for the conduct of serious warfare. Charles was even more annoyed by Parliament's refusal to vote him the right to collect tonnage and poundage (customs duties) for life, as had been granted to the monarch at the beginning of every preceding reign since the fifteenth century. The Commons would vote them for one year only; as the Lords refused to pass the bill in this restricted form it fell through altogether. Customs duties continued to be collected by prescriptive right, as they always had been after the death of a monarch until such time as a new Parliamentary grant could be made. It seemed at first to be a mere technicality posing no serious problems. Parliament was dissolved in August 1625, as soon as the impeachment of Buckingham appeared in the air.

There was as yet no thought of rule without Parliament and the second Parliament of the reign was called for February 1626. A clumsy attempt was made to castrate the opposition by appointing its leaders, notably Sir Edward Coke and Thomas Wentworth, as sheriffs so that they could not serve as Members of Parliament. But this move resulted in the initiative passing to the even more extreme Sir John Eliot. It is a good illustration of Charles's naïve view that all opposition could be ascribed to a

few factious individuals, and that once these 'agitators' were removed, Parliament would support his policy with loyalty and docility.

The Parliament of 1626 repeated and exaggerated all the opposition of 1625, with good reason, for the disastrous results of Buckingham's conduct of affairs were now becoming apparent. Buckingham was again the all-important issue: Parliament insisted that they would vote money only if he were removed. Charles obstinately refused, not only because of his personal attachment to the favourite, but also because he regarded the issue as one of principle and would not allow Parliament to dictate his choice of advisers. Charles's address to the Lords and Commons at Whitehall in 1626 is a revealing document, marked by the tones of personal affront he adopted in his relations with Parliament:

> You may remember that in the time of my Blessed Father you did with your Counsel and persuasion prevail with my father and me to break off the treaties [with Spain]. . . . Now that you have all

Ships from Buckingham's fleet in 1627. In 1627 Charles and Buckingham added to the war with Spain a much more dangerous one with France.

things according to your wishes, and I am so far engaged that you think there is no retreat, now you begin to set the dice and make your own game. But I pray you be not deceived: it is not a Parliamentary way, nor is it a way to deal with a King. Master Coke told you, it was better to dye by a foreign enemy than to be destroyed at home. Indeed I think it is more honour for a king to be invaded and almost destroyed by a foreign enemy, than to be despised by his own subjects. Remember that Parliaments are altogether in my own power for their calling, sitting, and dissolution; therefore as I find the fruits of them Good or Evil, they are to continue or not to be. And Remember that if in this time instead of mending your Errors, by delay you persist in your Errors, you make them greater and irreconcilable: whereas, on the other side, if you do go on cheerfully to mend them, and look to the distressed state of Christendom, and the Affairs of the Kingdom as it lyeth now by this great Engagement, you will do yourselves honour, you shall encourage me to go on with Parliaments.

This arrogant tone could hardly have been better designed to foster opposition and to silence those who might have been

*'I scorn
to threaten any
but my equals'*

willing to offer support. Perhaps it was because he was not really a strong and domineering character that Charles felt it so necessary to assert these sweeping theoretical claims of what was due to his royal majesty. He seems not to have realised what a bad impression was created by his tactlessness. The supreme example of this came when, after a similar harangue to his third Parliament, he ended with 'Take not this as threatening, for I scorn to threaten any but my equals.'

The second Parliament was dissolved in August 1626, without having voted supply, once again to prevent the impeachment of Buckingham. Men said with justice that 'Charles placed him in the balance against the whole Nation.' One reason for the decision to dissolve Parliament rather than allow the impeachment to proceed was that a strong opposition party existed in the Lords as well as in the Commons. This was in part the result of a quarrel between Charles and Buckingham on the one hand, and John Digby, Earl of Bristol on the other. Digby had been a close adviser of James, and involved in the Spanish marriage negotiations from the beginning. Charles and Buckingham had seized on him as a scapegoat for their own incompetence in this affair, and a quarrel had ensued which culminated in Charles levying the ridiculous accusation that Digby had tried to convert him to Popery while he was in Madrid. This was just one example of the way in which personal rivalries and intrigues at the top of the social pyramid were a vital element in the difficulties faced by the Crown in the 1620s. Government was still partly 'feudal' in the sense that the King needed to maintain a balance between the great lords, the men whose great wealth and lands afforded them a strong political position. They no longer took their armed retainers out to fight in their quarrels but, in the law courts, in Parliament, and in the competition for places, pensions and grants at Court, the same kind of rivalries were expressed. It was a world in which, at all levels of society, a 'masterless man' was in a weak and exposed position. The wise sought a protector. Parliament was only one of the fields of operation for this system of patronage and protection; the legal system and the royal Court were others.

In a sense the great struggle played out between the King and his barons from the time of King John and earlier was continued in the reigns of James and Charles. Under this system the King had a strong hand: he had many advantages, those of the un-defined royal prerogative, and as a great landowner in his own right. As the dispenser of all sorts of other grants and favours, wardships, patents of monopoly, licences of this and that, the King had far more to offer than any private citizen. But he needed to know how to play his cards. It was not good tactics for one royal favourite, himself despised as a *parvenu* and in-competent statesman, to monopolise the royal favour to the extent allowed by James and Charles. Support should have been forthcoming to Buckingham in return for all the favours he dispensed, but he never seems to have begun to realise how to organise it. He was too arrogant and blatantly selfish, demand-ing a high degree of obsequiousness from favoured ones, but ready to sacrifice them for temporary advantage. This was demonstrated in the cases of Mompesson, Bacon and then Middlesex.

Failure to obtain a Parliamentary grant to finance the war resulted in the resort to all sorts of expedients, which rapidly caused resentment. Forced loans were imposed on landowners, troops were billeted on the civil population, and the seaports were made to pay for the fleet. Several members of the gentry and nobility refused to pay the forced loan on principle and were imprisoned; the judges refused to apply a writ of *habeas corpus* in such cases. But an efficient bureaucracy would have been necessary to apply these measures and Charles did not have one. At the price of considerable unrest, only a small quantity of money was produced. The English governmental system, lacking the armies of royal officials on whom the French king could rely, needed the gentry's voluntary co-operation. Charles reverted to the alternative policy of looking for Parliamentary support, and his third Parliament was summoned in March 1628.

This time Wentworth and Coke were not excluded, and they returned to lead the opposition in the Commons. They deter-mined to ground their protest, not merely against Buckingham, but on general resistance to the arbitrary methods of govern-ment which Charles had employed for the past two years. This was expressed in the Petition of Right, which declared that the use of martial law on civilians, the forced billeting of troops, taxation without the consent of Parliament, and arbitrary

The death of Buckingham, Van Dyck's painting of the dead favourite. Buckingham's assassination in August 1628 allowed the return to Court of many of Charles's leading opponents in Parliament, among them Thomas Wentworth.

George Villiers,
Duke of Buckingham
(assassinated 1628)
by Vandyck.

imprisonment, were illegal. The Petition was endorsed by the Lords, and Charles was offered five subsidies if he agreed to it. Charles made obvious his reluctance to do so, by seeking to give assent by his 'royal word' that he would follow its provisions. But the opposition insisted that assent be given in the regular form of a private bill. It was all too obvious that Charles's word of honour meant nothing at all. In the end, facing further military defeats, Charles agreed to the Petition of Right on 7 June 1628. As there was no regular precedent for such a Petition, Charles tried to give his assent in a vague form: 'The King willeth that right be done according to the laws and customs of the realm'; but the opposition insisted on the regular form of assent to a private bill, '*soit droit fait comme est désiré*'. But this did not improve relations between King and Parliament as the opposition at once renewed the attack on Buckingham; they also embarked on an assault on the royal religious position by impeaching Roger Manwaring, a clergyman who had declared that to refuse the forced loans was to defy God as well as the King. Parliament was prorogued.

In August 1628 the question of Buckingham was to be removed from the Parliamentary agenda by his assassination at Portsmouth, where he was awaiting embarkation to join the army on the Ile de Ré. Buckingham's murderer was called John Felton, an unbalanced lieutenant, unconnected with the Parliamentary opposition. Recently disbanded from the navy without his pay, he had been carried away by the hysterical mixture of anti-Popery and anti-Buckingham feeling. Buckingham's assassination was in many ways like the crisis in a tragic drama: it at once reduced the political tension. The most tangible reason for opposition to the King was removed and Charles, freed from Buckingham's fatal spell, soon adopted more sensible foreign policies, making peace with France and Spain. Though he retained a vague idea of intervention in European politics to restore the Palatinate to his brother-in-law, he now sought this by diplomacy and intrigue, recognising the futility of military operations with the resources at his disposal.

The disappearance of Buckingham allowed the return to Court of several opposition leaders of the past three years, and this was also important. Most notable among them were Lord Bristol, Lord Arundel and Thomas Wentworth, the leading

Parliamentarian of 1625–8 now raised to the peerage as Viscount Wentworth, and created Lord President of the Council of the North. No longer was there one favourite, monopolising royal favours and having sole access to the royal ear, but a return to the old system of a Privy Council in which several great lords and advisers debated questions of policy. Their deliberations, however unsuccessful, at least produced sounder policy than Buckingham's brainwaves. In the summer of 1628, a red-faced irascible little cleric, William Laud, was promoted from a small bishopric to the important see of London, and the 'Laudian' programme for the reformation of the Church of England was initiated.

The transition was not immediate. Conflict continued in the summer and autumn of 1628 and there was further trouble when Parliament reassembled in January 1629. The extremists, led by Sir John Eliot, now moved against the King on religious grounds. The appointments made in the Church in the summer and autumn of 1628 marked a definite hardening of the line against Puritan tendencies in the Church. Charles issued a declaration in December 1628 that Parliament had no right to meddle in Church affairs. This was to seek a showdown, and it came in 1629, when the actions of the opposition in the Commons did much to alienate moderate opinion, and to prepare the way for acquiescence in the subsequent period of absolute rule.

The two issues of religion and finance were closely intermingled. The House had brought before it royal officials who had levied tonnage and poundage. Charles forbade questioning of his servants and ordered the Speaker to adjourn the House. This produced the famous scene of 2 March when two strong young members of Parliament forcibly held down the Speaker in his chair. He dissolved into tears and refused to put the three opposition resolutions to the vote. Completely losing his temper, Eliot threw the prepared text into the fire and a supporter, Denzil Holles, had to recite it from memory. This he did, while Black Rod knocked at the door unanswered and the King threatened to send royal guards to disperse the House. Before the doors were opened and the members dispersed, not to reassemble for eleven years, they declared the three resolutions passed by acclamation. In fact it is likely that had a regular vote

Denzil Holles Baron of Ifield married 5 Wifes
1. Dorothy & Heir
to Sr. Fr Ashley by
whch he had 4 Sons
2 Jane Eldest Daughter
& Coheir to Sr Jn Shirley
3 Hesther the
Second Daughter
& Coheir to Gideon
le Lou Lord of
the Mannor
of Columbiers
in Normandy
Dyd Ocbr. 31t.
1677
Aged 79.

LEFT Denzil Holles, one of the King's leading opponents in the House of Commons.
RIGHT Sir John Eliot, the great defender of the liberties and privileges of Parliament. In March 1629 he was imprisoned in the Tower after his resolutions against illegal taxation and innovations in religion had been recited in the House of Commons by Denzil Holles. Eliot's confinement in the Tower was exceptionally severe and he remained in prison until his death in the autumn of 1632.

been taken the resolutions would not have been carried. They declared:

(1) Whosoever shall bring in innovation of religion, or by favour or countenance seem to extend or introduce Popery or Arminianism or other opinion disagreeing from the true and orthodox Church, shall be reputed a capital enemy to this kingdom and commonwealth.

(2) Whosoever shall counsel or advise the taking and levying of the subsidies of tonnage and poundage, not being granted by Parliament, or shall be an actor or instrument therein, shall be likewise reputed an innovator in the government and a capital enemy to the kingdom and commonwealth.

RIGHT The central panel of the ceiling of Inigo Jones's Banqueting House at Whitehall which Charles I commissioned Rubens to paint. It represents the apotheosis of James I.

BELOW The magnificent Double Cube room, designed by Inigo Jones at Wilton House, the home of the Pembroke family. William, Earl of Pembroke was Lord Steward and his brother Philip, Lord Chamberlain to Charles I. Charles and Henrietta Maria, 'loved Wilton above all places and went there every summer'.

(3) If any merchant or person whatsoever shall voluntarily yield or pay the said subsidies of tonnage and poundage, not being granted by Parliament, he shall likewise be reputed a betrayer of the liberties of England, and an enemy to the same.

Although the 1629 Parliament was later described as a great step on the road to the destruction of royal power, its effect at the time was the reverse. The opposition had gone too far, and moderate men were alienated and more sympathetic to the King than they had been in 1628. Many of the opposition joined the King's side, among whom lawyers such as William Noy, who became Attorney General, Thomas Digges and Sir Edward Littleton were prominent. There would be no evolution, in the sense desired by Coke, to a position in which the judges asserted their right to determine whether the King's actions were constitutional. All the decisions of the 1630s, from the refusal to free Sir John Eliot, imprisoned in 1629 by royal command in the Tower until his death in 1632, to the decision against Hampden in the ship money case, were for the King. They were consistent with the rapid evolution of a Continental system of absolutism on the basis of English Common Law. The prerogative courts with their special powers were an additional card in the royal hand, but the Common Law itself was not repugnant to the growth of royal absolutism if the political context were favourable.

The death of Buckingham facilitated, if it was not directly responsible for, another turning point in Charles's life. This was his reconciliation with his Queen. Henrietta Maria had matured rapidly in the three years that she had been in England. She was ready to fall in love with Charles when he turned to her in his misery after Buckingham's death. Throughout his life Charles needed one individual on whom he could place complete trust and who would engage his affections entirely. Now he turned to his wife, and found that she was a very different person from the unhappy child that had met him at Dover in 1625. They remained united in their devotion to each other until Charles's death. If his love for his wife is one of the most attractive aspects of Charles's character as a private man, it was to turn out, in the crisis years after 1640, to be one of his worst political handicaps. He is said to have taken some of his most unfortunate decisions because of his over-anxiety about her physical safety. She sought to help her husband by engaging in political intrigue which had uniformly disastrous results, and he was never strong enough or sure enough of his own judgment to put a stop to these activities. Finally, her very existence as an avowed Roman Catholic was a severe political liability, however strong and sincere Charles's own Anglican faith.

The reconciliation of Charles and Henrietta Maria began in August 1628, immediately after Buckingham's death. In May 1629 she bore her first child, which died after a few hours. But this was followed twelve months later by a boy, who lived to become King Charles II. Henrietta Maria and Charles had eight children, born between May 1630 and June 1644. Prince Charles was followed by a sister, Mary, born in November 1631, who was to marry William II, Prince of Orange; then came James, later King James II, in 1633, and Elizabeth, born in 1635 who died as an adolescent. Two more girls were born, Anne in 1637, who died in 1641, and Catherine in 1639, then a boy, Henry, in 1640, and finally a girl, Henrietta, in 1644. Henrietta Maria had not been strikingly beautiful when she married Charles but maturity brought her great elegance and charm. In spite of frequent child-bearing, portraits from the 1630s reveal her to have been a very attractive woman. The best feature of her face was her eyes, which, changing from sparkling merriment to more solemn feeling, betrayed her emotional temperament. She soon developed fluent English, and gave a touch of gaiety to the Court, in contrast to Charles's rather solemn reserve.

Charles was chaste from first to last, and had eyes for his wife alone. Henrietta Maria called herself, in a letter to her French relations shortly after her reconciliation with Charles, 'the happiest woman in the world'. Although portraits of Charles always gave him a melancholy look, it is probably true that he would have regarded himself as the happiest husband in the world. Certainly these years from 1629 to 1637, with Charles in his thirties, were the happiest years of his life. He had matured late, but now the uncertainties and difficulties of adolescence were behind him and, secure sn his love for Henrietta Maria and for his growing family, he no longer needed a favourite. No other adviser ever had the personal hold over Charles that

OPPOSITE Queen Henrietta Maria, painted by Van Dyck in 1632 and placed in the King's bed-chamber at Whitehall.

66

The five eldest children of
Charles I, (from left to
right) Princess Mary,
Prince James, Prince
Charles, Princess Elizabeth
and Princess Anne. The
picture was painted by
Van Dyck for their parents
in 1637 and was placed
over the table in the King's
Breakfast Chamber
at Whitehall.

Jeffery Hudson, Queen Henrietta Maria's dwarf, by Daniel Mytens. The son of a butcher at Oakham, he was introduced to the Duchess of Buckingham at the age of nine. She released him from a pie at a dinner given for Charles and Henrietta Maria, who took him into her service. His adventurous career included a period of enslavement by Barbary pirates.

Buckingham had had. His ministers, Weston, Wentworth, Laud and the others were respected for their professional competence in their respective fields, but were not intimate personal friends. Although the formalities of Court life meant that the King and Queen were often separated, Charles sought as much as possible to be with her. Charles's looks, like those of his wife, improved with advancing years. His face remained rather immobile and solemn, with its heavy-lidded eyes and regular features. He was obviously not a man with much sense of humour. His chestnut hair began to have silver streaks in it before he was thirty. But his long, wistful face, had developed by this time a rather effeminate handsomeness. The tight lines of his mouth betrayed the nervous tension under which he played his role in the world.

4
The King Rules
Alone
1629-40

CHARLES HAD REASONS for satisfaction. After the foreign war and domestic conflict of his first four years as King, a great quietness descended over the land. Political conflict seemed to have been ended. Sir John Eliot was safely in the Tower; many of the leaders of the Parliamentary opposition, like Noy and Wentworth, had been brought into the royal service and were faithful servants of the Crown; other opponents were living quietly on their country estates and nothing was heard of them. It was true that finance still posed a problem, but then there was nothing new or unusual about that and the problem was certainly not acute. As long as peace was preserved, there seemed no reason why the Crown should not keep its head above water financially speaking. It would be wrong to regard the various devices for raising money that were resorted to in these years as desperate expedients. They were varied and ingenious, but were no more than the normal result of financial problems at that time and not the sign of a desperate financial plight. Apart from the income from what remained of the Crown lands, the main source of revenue was tonnage and poundage. There was trade depression in the 1630s causing some financial difficulty to the Crown, but the situation was not critical. The yield from the customs duties increased from an annual average of £260,000 in 1631–5 to an average of £400,000 in 1636–41. As long as they could be collected without protest and trade remained buoyant, there was no need to fear bankruptcy. As that was the case, it was easy enough to follow the habit of governments from medieval times to our own, and borrow. Until the crisis of 1639 the royal credit was good and Charles could borrow easily from the City financiers, from great noblemen and from groups such as the 'farmers' of the customs, to whom the collection of customs was leased. One of the main advantages of the 'farmers' was that they paid in advance, a system that might have developed, as it did in eighteenth-century France, into a massive public debt.

Certainly Charles cannot have felt himself unduly short of money in the 1630s. If his Court was not lavish by contemporary standards, such as those set in France or even those set by his father's Court, Henrietta Maria had expensive tastes and they do not seem to have been restricted unduly by her husband. The visit of her mother, Marie de Médicis, was an occasion of

PREVIOUS PAGES Charles I and Henrietta Maria departing for the chase, by Daniel Mytens.

considerable expense. Charles himself spent a great deal as a patron of the arts, both in encouraging living artists such as Van Dyck, and in making a magnificent collection of Italian pictures of the previous century. If it had not been dispersed during the Interregnum this would have provided London with one of the best collections of High Renaissance art made by any of the royal Houses of Europe. His taste in art was wide, extending to the Flemish and Spanish painters, as well as the Italians; it was also good. He bought masterpieces by Titian and Mantegna, and the famous Raphael cartoons. Among contemporaries he employed Rubens and Van Dyck, while Inigo Jones was the designer of scenery and costumes for the court masques in which the Queen delighted. At his death his collection included fourteen hundred pictures and four hundred pieces of sculpture.

Apart from his interest in painting and sculpture, Charles liked to listen to music and to attend plays and masques. His other great enjoyment was hunting, to which, like most noble-men and gentlemen of the period, he devoted a great deal of time. But he was not merely a man of pleasure. Even in the 1630s, in the quietest time of his reign, he spent a good deal of time on government business. Professor C. V. Wedgwood has complained that he was lazy and did not devote enough atten-tion to these tedious matters. There are plenty of indications, however, in the official documents, that Charles was personally involved in administration on a day to day basis and decided very important matters as well as questions of trivial detail. The nineteenth-century editor of the *Calendar of State Papers* for this period, J. Bruce, wrote that:

> Since Buckingham's death, King Charles had become well versed in business, was informed of whatever was going on, attended meetings, even of committees, directed their decisions, and, when not present, was consulted in all important matters. The government was really and truly his, not by a complimentary official figment, but by actual interference with its management and direction.

Charles was thus concerned in many different areas of policy, and among them foreign affairs played a major part. Although Charles was unable to follow a very effective line of action, at least he kept England at peace. He dabbled in various unlikely schemes, designed mainly to recover the Palatinate for his sister's family, but he had sense enough never to push things to the point of war. In domestic policy the government interfered in all sorts of ways, attempting to regulate economic life at a detailed level. One motive for this intervention was financial. Charters, privileges, and monopolies were always intended to produce revenue for the Crown; but other purposes were also served and there are signs that had absolute rule continued for a generation, intervention in the economic life of England might have eventually reached the level that it did in France under Colbert. It has been argued that these actions amounted to a paternalistic policy of intervention in economic life so as to defend the poor against exploitation by the rich, and that in this way Charles's absolute rule can be seen as an example of traditional 'feudal' kingship, which sought the welfare of the lower classes, and was therefore opposed by the selfish rich who triumphed in the Civil War. This interpretation strains the available evidence. Charles was, no doubt, a high-minded and conscientious King, who would always have said that he sought the welfare of all his subjects, including the poorest. But the way government worked in the early seventeenth century meant that State intervention usually led to good profits for some individual or privileged group, paid for by giving the King his share. There was no consistent policy of intervention in favour of the poor against the rich and the King was willing

During the 1630s, Charles repaired and strengthened the Navy, helped by the imposition of the tax known as ship money.
RIGHT The Dominion of the Sea Medal by Nicolas Briot struck in 1630, the year that the Treaty of Madrid brought peace with Spain.
OPPOSITE Peter Pett and the *Sovereign of the Seas*. This magnificent ship was built from the proceeds of ship money and launched in 1637. Peter Pett was Surveyor of the Navy at the time.

Inigo Jones

Inigo Jones, one of England's greatest architects and the founder of English classicism, occupied a position as arbiter of taste and the arts at the Court of Charles I. Appointed head of the King's Works in 1615 by James I, he retained this position under Charles until the outbreak of the Civil War brought an end to his activites.

RIGHT Drawing of Inigo Jones by Van Dyck.
BELOW The Queen's House at Greenwich designed by Inigo Jones; it was begun in 1616 for Charles's mother, Anne of Denmark, and completed for Henrietta Maria in 1635.

Inigo Jones's first
employment at Court was
as a designer of Court
masques. For many years
he collaborated with the
poet Ben Jonson to
produce a dazzling series of
entertainments, until the
two men quarrelled in 1631
and Jonson as a result lost
his royal patronage.
RIGHT and BELOW
Costume designs and
scenery by Inigo Jones for
Salmacida Spolia,
written by Sir William
D'Avenant; it was the last
masque to be performed at
Whitehall before the
Civil War.

Varieties of religious beliefs from a contemporary pamphlet. The broad Elizabethan Church settlement had encouraged the spread of different religious practices and beliefs.

to support drastic action against the traditional rights of the poor, as in his agreement to the schemes of the big capitalists who wanted to drain the fens, ousting those who lived by hunting and fishing in the marshes, and selling the land to rich landlords. In general, the rich merchants and financiers of London supported the King: for one reason, the King had borrowed large sums of money from them, and even as late as November 1641 they demonstrated their support for Charles by a joyful ceremonial reception on his return from Scotland.

Apart from foreign policy and the eternal question of revenue raising, the principal concern of Charles's administration in the eleven years of personal rule, as the period between 1629 and Charles's next Parliament in 1640 are known, was the govern-

Arian   Adamite   Libertin

Familist   Seeker   Divorcer

ment of the Church and matters of religion. Charles said, during his negotiations about the terms on which he could be restored to the throne after the first Civil War, that 'Men are ruled more by the pulpit than by the sword.' This was the universal opinion at the time, and for that reason religion was seen as an essential concern of the State. Not that Charles saw religion merely as a useful tool of government. He was sincerely and devoutly religious, and sought to impose a new 'beauty of holiness' on the forms of worship used in his kingdoms. He did this first in England, and then, with disastrous results, in Scotland. Religious motives were thoroughly intertwined with political motives in Charles's Church policy. He sought to impose a particular form of worship both for its own sake and because

Enter the Bishop of Canterbury, and with him a Do
Lawyer, and a Divine; who being set downe, they brin
of Dishes to his Table,

CAnterbury, is here all the dishes, that are provided
    Doct. My Lord, there is all : and 'tis enough, wer
Ther's 24. severall dainty dishes, and all rare.

    B, Cant. Are these rare : no, no, they please me not,
Give me a Carbinadoed cheek, or a tipper of a Cocks
None of all this, here is meate for my Pallet.

    Lawyer. My Lord, here is both Cocke and Phesant

A Puritan satire showing Laud dining off Prynne's
ears, which had been cropped as punishment for
Prynne's attack on the episcopal system of
Church government.

a Princes table,

be :

it had political implications. Even more, opposition to the King's views on religion clearly had political implications. In a letter to his eldest son, written shortly before he died, which he gave to Bishop Juxon on the day of his execution, Charles gave his account of the causes of the Civil War. In his eyes the root of the trouble was Presbyterianism:

> Nothing seemed less considerable than the Presbyterian faction in England for many years, so compliant they were to public order: nor, indeed was their party great either in Church or State as to men's judgements: but as soon as discontents drove men into sidings, as ill humours fall to the disaffected part, which causes inflammations, so did all at first who affected any novelties adhere to that side, as the most remarkable and specious note of difference (then) in point of religion. . . . Let nothing seem little or despicable to you in matters which concern religion and the Church's peace, so as to neglect a speedy reforming and effectually suppressing errors and schisms: what seems at first but a handbreadth, by seditious spirits, as by strong winds, are soon made a cover and darken the whole heaven.

By that time Charles had adopted the view expressed earlier by Laud who called Puritanism 'a wolf held by the ears'. In the 1630s, although Charles mainly supported Laud's policies for eradicating Puritanism, he had no real sense of crisis and danger. His policies were not strong enough or consistent enough really to crush the opposition to the Laudian system, but they were harsh enough to arouse formidable resentment, as in the famous case of Burton, Bastwick and Prynne. The affair of these three Puritans was typical of Charles's personal government. They were punished for publishing attacks on the episcopal system of Church government by being placed in the pillory, branded with the letters S.L. for 'seditious libeller', having their ears cropped, and being imprisoned. But they were allowed to make speeches in defence of their ideas from the pillory, and the barbarous punishment, instead of humiliating the victims, made them martyrs and created widespread hostility to the government.

Many who were not themselves much concerned about theology found much that was disquieting in Charles's religious policy. It was enforced through the prerogative courts, the Star Chamber and High Commission, which were given

William Laud

Laud, the son of a Reading clothier, entered the Church in 1601 and rapidly obtained advancement. He early took up a position of antagonism to the Calvinistic party in the Church and on the accession of Charles his activities were allowed freer scope. His powers were extended further when he became Archbishop of Canterbury in 1633 and he proceeded to impose the religious ceremonies and usages to which he attached so much importance. Unimaginative, outspoken and rude, Laud had many enemies, and he was particularly hated in London for his merciless persecution of the Puritans. However, the University of Oxford, where Laud carried out many useful reforms, remembers him with kindness.

BELOW 'Triple Episcopacie' – a contemporary satire on Laud and the Court bishops, produced by the Puritans. Laud thought he was aiming at an English 'moderation' in the tradition of Matthew Parker, John Whitgift and Richard Hooker, but he was mistrusted for his 'popish superstitious practices'.

RIGHT Archbishop Laud, a portrait from the studio of Van Dyck.

Of God,   Of Man,   Of the Divell.

OPPOSITE The interior of Inigo Jones's Queen's Chapel at St James's Palace, begun for the Infanta Maria in 1623 and finished for Henrietta Maria in 1627. The existence of a Roman Catholic chapel at Court, attended by Henrietta Maria and her entourage, strengthened the fear that England was moving closer to Popery.

greater authority at the expense of the Common Law courts. With Laud, now Archbishop of Canterbury, and Bishop Juxon of London as prominent members of the King's Council, administering civil as well as ecclesiastical affairs, it seemed that clerical government was returning in a way that had not been known since the Reformation. Laud's desire to restore some of the wealth of the Church that had been lost through generations of lay encroachment on tithes and other Church income and property, was especially worrying to men of property. In Scotland also this sort of question brought many rich landowners who had little theological quarrel with Laud, to cast their lot for Presbyterianism and the Covenant. But in the last resort it was not the financial question that made religion such a potent source of opposition. Religion touched on much deeper emotions, especially when it became involved with international questions.

Although Charles was a devout Protestant, and Laud was equally convinced that the Church of England was in the true Catholic tradition, far removed from the aberrations of Roman Catholicism, in a crude way the Laudian movement could be represented as trying to divert the Church of England back to Romish practices. Laud's insistence on such things as placing the communion-table at the east end of the church, like the traditional altar of the Roman Catholics, and not in the middle of the congregation, and the return to other ceremonial practices, seemed to some like a half-way house to Popery. The existence of a Roman Catholic chapel at Court, attended by Henrietta Maria and her entourage, and the presence there of papal representatives, strengthened the feeling that the Protestant religion was endangered. Charles's foreign policy, which by now leaned towards Spain, was also a source of disquiet. He even went so far as to help the Spaniards send money to the Netherlands to pay their soldiers there. As the Thirty Years' War was still being fought and could be interpreted as a continuation of the century-old struggle between Protestantism and Catholicism, there were several reasons for the development of the hysterical atmosphere which pushed the country into civil war. Men feared the triumph of Catholicism in Europe and Charles seemed to be an ally of the Catholic powers. It only needed the panic produced by the Catholic rising against

the Protestant settlers in Ireland to complete the development of a situation which led to war.

Charles's decision to rule without Parliament used to be described as leading to 'the eleven-year tyranny'. In this interpretation it was assumed that a constitutional system of government, based on Parliament, already existed and was challenged by Charles. This is clearly not the case. The dichotomy between constitutional and unconstitutional does not make much sense when applied to the early seventeenth century. It only emerged in the course of the crisis of 1640–2. But the pendulum has swung too far the other way in recent interpretations, which state that Charles was doing nothing unusual in these years. Although the claims of the Parliamentary opposition at the time, later repeated by the Whig historians, that Parliamentary government had existed in complete and perfect form in the Middle Ages, are obviously false, it would be equally naïve to accept what amounts to Charles's own view.

'We shall account it presumption for any to prescribe any time unto us for Parliaments'

He claimed that Parliaments were for him to call or not as he thought fit and that there was no need to call them if he did not wish to do so. This was, of course, the situation in strictly legal terms, but in political terms it was unwise to take this view in 1629. Charles was never able to see that what might seem to be the most advantageous interpretation of the legal position, itself confused and ambiguous, was not wise politically. The House of Commons had already been making bigger political claims in the reign of Elizabeth and this process had continued under James I. From 1621 to 1629 there had been frequent Parliaments, and the intensity of their opposition to the King had grown from year to year. Charles's decision in 1629, if not as revolutionary as the opposition party claimed, was a considerable breach with tradition. It cannot be said, as some have done, that there was nothing of a challenge in Charles's actions: in the Proclamation of Dissolution, in his speech to the Lords and in the Royal Declaration, Charles issued a statement of his case against the Commons, implying that he was going to move the balance back towards royal power. If the King's programme after 1629 had been successful it might perhaps have ended by taking England down the road that produced royal absolutism in Continental states.

There is a good deal of truth in the Whig view that under

88

Elizabeth and James there had been developing a form of government with the consent of the people – if by people we mean the politically dominant, landowning class, the gentry. Charles was now to embark on the experiment of ruling against them, without their consent, without Parliament. There is no sense in calling this unconstitutional: it was not clear then what was constitutional and what was not. But it was a programme that was bound to produce resistance, in spite of the deceptive quiescence of the first few years.

The absence of Parliament allowed Charles to get more and more out of touch with the dominant opinion of the majority of his subjects. As a result he destroyed the fund of goodwill that he had obtained by the extremism of the opposition in 1629. By insisting on his absolute power, he gradually produced a sort of 'strike' among the gentry, whose co-operation was needed for the work of administering the country. The argument over ship money is a good example of how Charles could be legally right and politically wrong. This tax had been traditionally levied on the seaports at times of emergency for the specific purpose of strengthening the navy. It was obviously sensible to affirm that the Crown had the right to demand money for national defence, and to state that the King alone was the judge of whether or not there was an emergency. Ship money had not provoked serious opposition when it was levied only on seaports, and thus had been paid mainly by the merchant class who could see the advantage of having a royal navy to protect commerce from pirates and enemies. But when the attempt was made to extend it to the whole country, opposition began. It was *not* politically sensible for Charles to try to turn ship money into a new and general land tax. Even if the amounts demanded were relatively modest, once the principle had been established they could later be increased, and the precedent of a direct tax on land, at the royal discretion, could have been established. Thus, John Hampden, a rich Buckinghamshire landowner, one of the immortal names in the struggle for British liberties and a member of the group which had already opposed the King in Parliament, refused to pay, and fought the case in the courts. The judges decided in favour of the King, but only by a narrow majority. It was typical of Charles's legalism and political incompetence that he should have seen this decision

JOHN HAMPDEN,
A·D· 1643.

90

as a justification for his policy and not as a strong warning. Most landowners continued to pay ship money until the end of 1638 but resentment was growing, and passive resistance among the gentry class began to build up.

Charles showed how little he realised these dangers by his attempt to bring the Scottish Church into line with the Church of England. The first move was an attempt to strengthen the authority of the bishops in the Scottish Church, who had little control over their flocks. What really brought disaster was the decision to impose a new Prayer Book containing new forms of service closely akin to the English forms. This led to the famous riot in St Giles's Cathedral in Edinburgh during which a stool was thrown at the priest. By the summer of 1637, as Charles had refused to yield an inch, there was opposition throughout Scotland; by the spring of 1638 the National Covenant was signed by all classes of Scottish Protestants, rich and poor. The subscribers swore to resist the new innovations to the death and to defend by arms the right of the Scottish Church to decide in free assembly what religious changes could be made. It was too late to retreat now. Charles had refused to conciliate the Scots while there was still time, and his attempt to do so in 1638 only encouraged resistance. Macaulay stated that: 'Charles acted at this conjuncture as he acted at every important conjuncture throughout his life. After oppressing, threatening, and bluster-ing, he hesitated and failed. He was bold in the wrong place, and timid in the wrong place.' Scotland was out of control, and unless the opposition was crushed, Charles's prestige and authority would suffer an enormous blow. Thus the decision was taken to raise an English army to defeat the Scottish rebels, a decision that revealed not open opposition, but passive resis-tance to Charles in England as well.

The ramshackle machinery of Stuart government was forced into action and unwilling recruits were pressed into an army of sorts. Officered by gentry who were mostly as reluctant to fight as the rank and file, they moved slowly northwards, with Charles at their head, in the spring of 1639. A little aimless skir-mishing was ended by the Peace of Berwick in June 1639. Charles had done nothing except demonstrate his weakness to the Scottish opposition and to the English also. There can be little doubt that the two were soon in touch with each other.

OPPOSITE John Hampden. A wealthy Buckinghamshire landowner, his refusal to pay ship money in 1637 was a direct challenge to Charles's prerogative. In the famous trial which followed, only seven of the twelve judges sided against Hampden, but Charles foolishly did not recognise that this was a clear warning of the opposition that was building up against him. Hampden remained an enthusiastic Parliamentarian, and was killed in 1643 during the Civil War.

The famous riot in
St Giles's Cathedral,
Edinburgh, when a
footstool was thrown at
the priest who was reading
the new Prayer Book.

The Peace of Berwick was obviously only an armistice and both
sides sought to strengthen their forces for a resumption of the
struggle. Charles's most important act was to recall Thomas
Wentworth from Ireland, where he had been Lord Deputy
since 1632 and had gained the reputation of the 'strong man',
who was needed to deal with English and Scottish affairs. He
arrived in England on 22 September 1639 and from that
moment until his impeachment just over a year later he was
Charles's principal adviser. His domineering personality en-
sured that his was the overriding influence, and he must be held
responsible, as much as Charles, for the disastrous turn that
affairs took in the next twelve months.

Although Charles had consulted him by letter while he was in
Ireland, he had not at that time played a decisive role in policy
making. Charles did not have the affection for him that he had
had for Buckingham. Only one person now was the target for
his emotions in the way that Buckingham had been: the Queen.

Wentworth was not even a congenial companion. There can be no doubt that the strength of his personality, which put in the shade all others at the Court, meant that he was respected and feared but certainly not liked. Although Charles was intellectually convinced of the absolute nature of royal power, he was not really a ruthless despot; in Wentworth he found someone who was. Wentworth was one of the few English gentlemen of his age whose mode of thought was not dominated by the procedural niceties of the Common Law. If it had been possible to build royal absolutism in England, Wentworth would have been the man to do it. No one else at Court matched him in the ruthlessness with which he was prepared to dispense with legal forms and precedents, and rest the King's claim on that cynical French maxim '*La raison du plus fort est toujours la meilleure*', or colloquially, 'might is right'.

However, the crisis year of 1640 was to show that a strong hand was not enough. Wentworth, created Earl of Strafford in January 1640, was responsible for the fatal decision to call Parliament again. This might seem a paradoxical step, but it was not so in reality. The truth of the matter was that the absence of any real administrative system in England meant that government depended on the co-operation of the landowning gentry. It had been possible to muddle along without Parliament in the peaceable years of the 1630s, but a crisis could not be met without the recall of Parliament. This had been demonstrated by the fiasco of the first expedition against the Scots in 1639. It has been stated by F.C. Dietz that the Crown was not short of money in 1639, and that it was not financial pressure that forced the decision to call Parliament. However that may be, and it seems doubtful that the royal finances could have withstood a serious campaign, finance was only one aspect of the situation. Not shortage of money, but the gentry's refusal to co-operate had been responsible for the poor showing of the royal army in 1639. The gentry had to be persuaded to assist the King.

Strafford completely miscalculated the possibility of winning support for royal policies in the English Parliament. His idea was that, as in 1629, if Parliament were called, the extremists would discredit themselves and allow the King to appeal to moderate opinion, so that he could rule effectively with or without Parliament. Either the patriotic appeal for support against

Thomas Wentworth, Earl
of Strafford, dictating to
his secretary, by Van Dyck.

94

the Scots would be successful, or if not, Charles 'might have the wherewithal to justify himself to God and the world that in his own inclination he desired the old way', but that he could not allow 'the peevishness of some few factious spirits' to destroy his government. Before Parliament met, Strafford made a lightning visit to Dublin in March 1640, and won from the Irish Parliament the vote of four subsidies to pay for the raising of an army to be used against the rebellious Scots in Ulster and in Scotland. The fact that this army could also be used against rebellious subjects in England was to be one of the crucial charges against him when he was impeached.

As soon as Parliament assembled on 13 April 1640, it became obvious that the Commons were in no mood obediently to support the King against the Scots. The opposition in the English Parliament were in touch with the Scots, and both parties knew that they stood or fell together. Instead of voting twelve subsidies in return for the abandonment of the royal claim to levy ship money, Parliament embarked on a recitation of its grievances against the King. And it was this Parliament that saw the emergence of a leader of whom more was to be heard: John Pym, ablest of the Parliamentary tacticians, who welded the great majority of the House together in defence of the rights of Parliament against the Crown. When it became clear that Pym was in touch with the Scots and that he was preparing a petition against the Scottish war, Parliament was dissolved. As it had sat for less than a month it became known as the Short Parliament.

At a meeting of a special committee of eight members of the Royal Council at the time of the dissolution of the Short Parliament, Strafford argued that the King should now consider himself free from all legal restraints. His words were to be used as the principal element in the charges of treason brought against him a few months later, when his reference to the possibility of bringing the royal army in Ireland over to deal with 'this kingdom' was interpreted as meaning England instead of Scotland. Strafford's speech at this meeting was noted in these words by the Secretary:

> No defensive war; loss of honour and reputation. So on with a vigorous war, as you first designed, loose and absolved from all rules of government: being reduced to extreme necessity, everything is to be done that power might admit. . . . You have an army

in Ireland you may employ here to reduce this kingdom. Confident as anything under heaven that Scotland shall not hold out five months. One summer well employed will do it....

Although there was much tough talk from Strafford, it could not be said that there was any serious attempt to impose the tough policy he had pursued in Ireland on England. Only three members of Parliament were arrested. This was hardly the way to break the strength of the Parliamentary opposition, none of whose leaders was touched. Rioting in London was suppressed and two apprentices hanged, but when the aldermen refused to grant a new loan, Strafford's advice to encourage the others to open their purse strings by hanging a few, was not followed. 'Never came a man to so lost a business,' he ruefully reflected.

The King did not have the administrative machinery to rule the country against the gentry. Various expedients were tried to raise the money that was not forthcoming from Parliament, such as ship money and 'coat and conduct' money (demanded from the gentry for clothing and transporting the soldiers they had raised), both medieval precedents which were strained in their interpretation. They met with widespread resistance. Bailiffs and constables who were ordered to distrain upon the goods of those who refused to pay, replied that they were afraid to do so. Some of them replied that 'they had rather fall into the hands of his Majesty, than into the hands of resolute men'. Men were refusing to accept appointment as justices of the peace and the machinery of government was beginning to break down. There were serious disorders in several parts of the country. Only mutinous, unsoldierly levies began to move slowly northwards to meet the Scots. Even in Ireland, the vote of the Dublin Parliament was not transformed into an effective army that could be used against rebels, Scottish or English.

On 29 August 1640 the Scots, realising the weakness of their opponents, advanced across the Tyne, defeating the most advanced section of the English army; the remainder retreated precipitately to York, leaving the garrison of Newcastle with no alternative but to surrender. Without much loss of blood the Scots occupied the counties of Durham and Northumberland. Charles called a Great Council of the peerage at York, following vague medieval precedents. They advised him to call another Parliament and appointed a committee to negotiate with the

Scots at Ripon. The Treaty of Ripon was cleverly calculated to obtain the maximum leverage upon Charles. Not only did he have to accept what amounted to Scottish independence from royal control, in both political and religious matters, but in order to ensure that he was in no position to break his word the Scots enforced a large money indemnity. This could only be paid by a Parliamentary grant, and until payment was received the Scottish army would continue to occupy the northern counties. Once again the opposition to Charles in Scotland and in England showed that they realised their common interests. Bound hand and foot in this way to his English opponents, Charles would never again be free to levy war against his Scottish subjects.

Charles was now to reap the bitter fruits of changing from one tactic to another, and failing in both. He would have done far better to keep the Short Parliament, than to dissolve it and to fail so abjectly in the alternative policy of non-Parliamentary rule. In case anyone had forgotten, he had again demonstrated that he would only abide by the forms of Parliamentary rule if he was forced – hence the strength of the opposition in what became known as the Long Parliament. For the first year of its existence – from 3 November 1640 to November 1641 – only about a third of the members supported the King. Most of those who later fought for the King in the Civil War were at this time his opponents. Edward Hyde, in 1661 created Earl of Clarendon, the later royal adviser and historian of the Civil War, was the most prominent of those who opposed Charles in 1641, only to return to his side when it became clear that the movement to restrict royal power was escalating into a revolution that would go far beyond any middle point, in both political and religious matters.

Castrum Royale Londinense, vulgo

5 From Peace

the TOWER

to War 1640-2

WHEN CHARLES RETURNED to London from York in October 1640 he was about to meet the great crisis of his reign. His actions in the subsequent fourteen months were the turning point of the reign, and one of the major turning points of English history. It was as a result of what he did and did not do in those months, that Charles lost the throne, and England embarked on the great experiment of non-monarchical rule, first as a temporary and unformulated expedient, and finally as an openly proclaimed 'Commonwealth' or Republic. Much was already a foregone conclusion in October 1640. It was already clear that absolute monarchy, of the sort that Charles had tried to set up in the previous ten years, could not be established in England. But the fact that events took such extreme courses, producing the Civil Wars and the complete, if temporary, extinction of the monarchy, was largely the result of Charles's handling of the situation.

One reason for the failure of Charles's policy at this time was that he was deprived of the advice of all the leading ministers on whom he had come to rely. Their achievements during the last eleven years may not have been brilliant, but Charles soon showed that without them he was helpless as a dismasted ship, drifting in a storm-tossed sea. The crucial step was the immediate impeachment of Strafford, a few days after the opening of Parliament, as soon as he returned to London. He was at once removed to custody in the Tower while the charges against him were prepared. Archbishop Laud followed him to the Tower in December, while the other leading ministers were frightened into flight and exile. The Secretary, Sir Francis Windebank, accused of protecting Catholics, fled in December, as did the Lord Keeper Finch. Other judges found themselves in a dangerous situation, as a result of having ruled in favour of Charles's interpretation of his prerogative power. The result was that Charles found himself without any of his most trusted advisers, although he was able from time to time to discuss political affairs with Strafford. For the first time Henrietta Maria began to play a direct part in political matters, a part which was to be uniformly disastrous. Deprived of other advice Charles listened to her. Totally unaware of the strength of feeling that had developed among the English gentry in defence of Parliamentary institutions and the Common Law, she encouraged

100

Charles in his belief that he could still rescue royal absolutism. This meant that he never consistently accepted the concessions that he was forced to make to Parliament, and continued to dabble with the idea of a *coup d'état* or of foreign intervention to restore him to his old power.

The other determining element in the situation was that, in the person of John Pym, Charles found himself opposed by a master of Parliamentary and political tactics. A West Country gentleman, born in 1584, and imbued with the anti-Spanish, anti-papal traditions of his youth, Pym had decided that Charles was not to be trusted. He was adamant in his belief that English liberty and the Protestant religion would be safe only if Charles were bound hand and foot, so that never again could he dispense with Parliament. Pym was not an extreme Puritan and he managed to keep the religious question in the background until what he regarded as essential had been first achieved. This was the removal of Charles's evil advisers, primarily Strafford, and the great series of legislative enactments that would make it impossible for Charles, or any successor, to rule without the co-operation of Parliament. It is not easy to decide whether or not Pym saw where the logic of his programme was taking him: a fully constitutional monarchy in which the King was a figure-head and in which political decisions were taken by ministers forced on the King, whether he wanted them or not, because they could command a majority in Parliament. At any rate, there was talk on more than one occasion during the first half of 1641 of a ministry to be formed by Pym and his friends, Hampden, Lord Saye, Lord Brooke, Denzil Holles and others. But nothing ever came of it, either because Pym refused, or because the King drew back, seeking other courses to extricate himself from his difficulties.

It would be easy to fall into the error of discussing the politics of 1641 in modern terms, seeing Pym as the leader of the majority party in the Commons who should have been called on to form a government. In reality things had not yet gone as far as that. Although Pym had a sure touch in the Commons, he could not control his followers in the way that, for example, a party leader of the nineteenth century could do. Pym and his friends did indeed meet to plan their tactics, and had used the Providence Island Company, of which he and a number of his

'Mr Pym, a man of good reputation'

OPPOSITE John Pym. He, more than any other man, provided the basis for Parliament's ultimate victory by his championship of Parliament's rights and his leadership of the Commons.

political friends were shareholders, as a way of keeping in touch during the period of non-Parliamentary rule. But they did not form anything which we can identify with a modern political party. Only a small number of members of Parliament were in close touch with Pym; he followed the majority almost as much as he led it, and it must never be forgotten that even the most important votes were taken while about half the members were absent.

Nevertheless, it was Pym and his friends who managed the Commons, and to a lesser extent, the House of Lords as well, if anyone did. It was certainly not the King. One way of looking at the evolution of relations between Crown and Parliament is to contrast the periods during which the Crown was able to manage Parliament, through judicious use of patronage and by taking appropriate policy decisions, with those periods in which the Crown lost control and allowed a clear-cut opposition between the Crown and Parliament to develop. Queen Elizabeth had been able, through the presence of important members of the Privy Council in the Commons, to exercise a good deal of control. In the eighteenth century it was complained that the power of the Crown, destroyed as prerogative, had grown up again in the form of 'influence' and for long periods there was no conflict. The Stuarts in the seventeenth century only rarely achieved this degree of control, and the last years of James's reign and the whole of Charles's are the extreme example of the Crown's failure to use its potential advantages, which still existed, to win support in Parliament. The first twelve months of the Long Parliament saw the nadir of royal influence in Parliament. Support for the King came only from a helpless minority, until the opposition went too far, and in the autumn of 1641 a Royalist party began to constitute itself.

One reason for this was the strange passivity in Charles's conduct of affairs throughout this period. He lent himself occasionally to various schemes for the restoration of his authority by force, and also tried conciliation. But conciliation, to be effective, would have had to be based on a sincere and whole-hearted acceptance of the claims of Parliament. Charles never gave that acceptance and he made it obvious that he did not. The inevitable result was to prolong the deadlock between himself and Parliament, a deadlock which he finally tried to

Master PYM

HIS SPEECH

In *Parliament*, on *Wednesday*, the
fifth of *January*, 1641,

Concerning the Vote of the House of *Commons*,
for his discharge upon the Accusation of High
Treason, exhibited against himselfe, and the
Lord *Kimbolton*, Mr. *Iohn Hampden*, Sr.
Arthur Haslerig, Mr: *Strowd*,
M. Hollis, by his Maiesty,

The true Effigies of Mr. *Iohn Pym*, Esquire

London Printed for I.W, 1641.

resolve by the gambler's throw of the attempted arrest of the five members of the House of Commons in January 1641; even if he had succeeded in this *coup* it is difficult to see how he could have improved his situation. It is a measure of Charles's failure to see the depth and extent of the antagonism towards him that he persisted in the belief that all would be well if he deprived the opposition of a few leaders.

Not much is known about any seventeenth-century elections, but it is clear that in spite of the importance of traditional local and family rivalries, the elections in the autumn of 1640 were in many instances fought on the issue of whether candidates were for or against the King. The result was a crushing defeat for the King. Even in such strongholds of royal patronage as the Duchies of Lancaster and Cornwall, official candidates had little success, and outright opponents were returned. Already in the spring elections to the Short Parliament, one poetical pamphleteer had written:

> Choose no ship sheriff or court atheist,
> No fen drainer nor church papist.

On 3 November Charles went to open Parliament not with the usual pomp and pageantry of a ceremonial procession, but by barge from Whitehall to Westminster stairs, and then on foot. The Venetian ambassador commented that this

> . . . shows more clearly than ever to his people that he consents to the summons merely from compulsion . . . and not of his own free will. . . . Thus instead of conciliating their good will at which he ought to aim particularly just now, he alienates them over a matter of outward show which is of no real importance, while at the same time he increases the admiration at the steps taken by the rebels, to whose bold resolution they do not tire of publishing their indebtedness for the re-establishment of liberty and religion alike.

Charles's opening speech was equally tactless: it centred on his immediate need for money to chase the rebels out of the kingdom. The Commons were indignant at his blunt use of the word 'rebels' to designate the Scots and were also insistant that redress of grievance must precede supply. It was foolish of Charles to imagine that they would grant him money to pay off the Scots before firmly establishing the rights of Parliament. The general opinion in the Commons was that expressed by Robert Baillie, the Scots' representative in London, that as long as the lads around Newcastle sat still there was nothing to worry about. Before they were induced to go home, the cause of liberty and religion in England must be rooted firm. That being so, Charles would have been well advised not to ask for the impossible. In fact he had to return two days later and make a more conciliatory speech.

One of the strangest features of the situation was the extent to which Charles let the initiative slip entirely from his hands, while the Commons, under the guidance of 'King Pym', as he came to be called in the pamphlet literature of 1641, proceeded to impeach his advisers and to prepare legislation to reform Church and State. Without Strafford to drive him on, the King allowed the weak side of his character to take charge and stood by while all who had served him were arrested or driven into exile. On 11 December 1640 Alderman Pennington, one of the members for the City of London, introduced a petition demanding the 'root and branch' abolition of episcopal government in the Church. That this attack on the Church Charles knew and loved was not for the moment pressed home was due to Pym's tactics. He did not want at that time prolonged discussion of religious questions which would divide the Commons. He diverted attention to a personal attack on Laud, leaving the question of the ideal future Church to the discussions of a committee. The House of Commons could not then, or at any time in the future, agree on how they wished to reform the Church, but they could agree on what they were against: the Laudian innovations and, above all, Laud himself.

Charles does not seem to have tried to interfere with the doings in Parliament. In spite of the ominous build-up of tension he was reported by the Venetian ambassador to be cheerful and optimistic, although the death of his four-year-old daughter must have added personal sorrow to the bitterness of political defeat. But Charles did not yet realise how great his defeat was to become. He brought off something of a diplomatic victory by marrying the nine-year-old Princess Mary to the young Prince William of Orange, son of the Stadtholder of Holland. The marriage might be expected to bring solid support from Holland if his relations with his rebellious subjects deteriorated further, although he was never in fact to get very much help from his Dutch relations.

Meanwhile Parliament was seeking to secure itself against any repetition of the period of personal rule by the passing of the Triennial Act, stating that a new Parliament must be called at least once every three years. Charles assented to this Act, with as bad a grace as possible, on 16 February 1641. In his speech to the Lords and Commons on that day he complained that in assenting to the Bill he was doing more than giving them the benefit of the doubt. They had not, he said, earned any such generosity from him, and he hoped that future Parliaments would be more co-operative than they had as yet been. He said:

> ... for, hitherto, to speak freely, I have had no great encouragement to do it: if I should look at the outward face of your actions, and not the inward intentions of your hearts, I might make question of doing it. Hitherto you have done what concerns yourselves, to amend and secure the things that are profitable to yourselves, neither were they things that merely concern the strength of this kingdom or the state in any one particular. This I mention not to reproach you, but to shew you the state of things as they are: you have taken the government almost to pieces, and, I may say, it is almost off the hinges. A skilful watchmaker to clean his watch takes it asunder, and when it is put together it will go better: but just remember if you leave out one pin the watch may be the worse and not the better.

Again, as Charles had decided to assent to the Bill he might as well have been less grudging in his acceptance. He still felt himself strong enough to reprieve a Catholic priest, condemned to death for the exercise of his religion, and he had no idea yet that he would be unable to save Strafford.

Strafford's trial began on 22 March in Westminster Hall, the great medieval hall adjacent to the Houses of Parliament. The medieval palace had long since been abandoned as a royal residence, and was used to house the judicial and administrative apparatus of the State. The Hall, which was to be the scene of Charles's own trial eight years later, was specially arranged so that large numbers of spectators could attend. There was a royal box, where the King and Queen were frequently to be seen. Strafford was an ill man and was given permission to keep his head covered with a fur-lined cap to protect him from the draughts of the vast room. He was impeached on the vague charge of 'endeavouring to subvert the fundamental laws and

OPPOSITE William of Orange and Princess Mary, by Van Dyck. Their marriage in April 1641 was a diplomatic *coup* for Charles, who thought he could rely on support from Holland in the event of armed confrontation in England.

government . . . and to introduce an arbitrary and tyrannical government against law'. Strafford himself, when he saw the charges, said that there was nothing in them on which he could legally be condemned to death. The most telling point against him rested on the remarks he had made on 5 May 1640 about using the Irish army 'to reduce this kingdom'. Notes of this meeting made by the secretary Sir Henry Vane had been leaked to the opposition by Vane's son, later to become a Republican and as such executed at the Restoration. But it was a firm point of law, even admitting the worst interpretation of the uncertain words, that a man could not be convicted of treason on the evidence of one man alone. Strafford presented his case with great logic and with the force of passionate conviction. He told his fellow peers, who by the procedure of impeachment were his judges, 'You, your posterity, are at stake.' If sincere advice to the King were to be presented as treason, how could anyone in the future accept the risk of joining the royal council:

> Do not, my lords, put such difficulties upon ministers of state that men of wisdom, of honour, of fortune, may not with cheerfulness and safety be employed for the public. If you weigh and measure them by grains and scruples, the public affairs of the kingdom will be waste. No man will meddle with them that hath anything to lose.

But although Strafford had the better of the argument, the opposition were determined that he should not escape. 'Stone dead hath no fellow', said the Puritan Earl of Essex, one of the leading opposition peers. Strafford was too dangerous a man to be allowed to live and possibly advise the King again. The procedure was changed from impeachment, in which the House of Lords acted as a court and normal legal rules had to be followed, to an Act of Attainder, in which an act of Parliament merely assigned an individual to death, without there being need for precise proof. The change also meant that Charles would have to take responsibility for Strafford's death. Impeachment proceeded without the royal assent, but an Act of Attainder needed the royal signature, like any other act of Parliament.

On 21 April the Bill passed its third reading in the Commons, and on the same day Charles gave Strafford his word of honour that he would not allow his execution. But the pressures that were to be brought on him were soon to render the promise worthless. Charles's desperate attempts to save Strafford only

Conf. Ship.

Land and Barkley. Lo. Tower.

Dep

'Old Newes Newly Revived', a broadsheet of 1641, satirising the downfall of
the King's friends and the King's policies. As soon as Parliament met in 1640, it launched
an attack on the King's ministers and many were frightened into flight and exile.

Strafford's Downfall

Thomas Wentworth had been an early opponent of Charles's policies in the House of Commons, but after the Petition of the Right in 1628, he joined the King's supporters and was created President of the Council of the North. In 1632 he was made Lord Deputy of Ireland and he arrived in Dublin in July 1633. There he pursued what he described as a policy of 'Thorough': he reformed the administration and the Church, and broke down the tyranny of the great lords over the poor. Yet these valuable measures were carried out by arbitrary means, and the fact he had raised an army for the prosecution of his Irish policy aroused the fear and anger of the Parliamentarians. As he was the most able and determined of the King's men, the Commons were convinced that his destruction was essential to the liberties of the kingdom.

The Earl of Strafford, after Van Dyck.

LEFT Strafford's trial in Westminster Hall, by Hollar. The procedure for the trial was changed from impeachment to a Bill of Attainder because of opposition from the House of Lords to the impeachment.

BELOW The execution of Strafford on Tower Hill. Charles never forgave himself for consenting to the death of the greatest of his servants, and towards the end of his own life, he said that his sufferings had come upon him as a punishment for permitting Strafford's death.

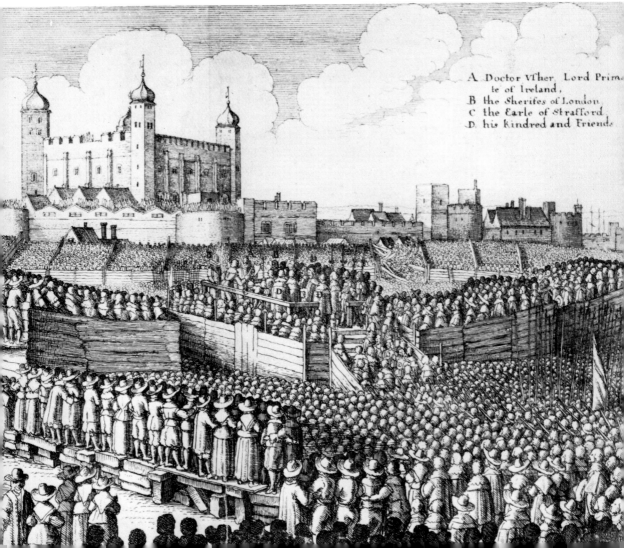

A Doctor Vsher Lord Primate of Ireland,
B the Sherifes of London
C the Earle of Strafford
D his kindred and Friends

made his death more inevitable. He swung from conciliation to repression, considering in the first few days of May a plan to bring Bedford, Pym, and some of the leading opponents, into office. The plan was dropped when Bedford died on 9 May. At the same time Charles continued to dabble with military plots, and sought in vain to put officers of assured loyalty in charge of the Tower. Revelations of the intrigues between the Court and certain army officers were used to great effect by Pym in the Commons on 5 May. Mob violence reached a previously unknown pitch, and was an important factor in assuring Strafford's condemnation by the Lords, and then in forcing the King's reluctant decision not to veto the Bill. On 1 May Charles addressed the Lords, telling them that he would never again employ Strafford 'in any place of nearness or trust', but that his conscience would not allow him to sign the Act of Attainder. This was the weakest of arguments, and encouraged the Lords to pass the Bill, safe in the assurance that it would be of no effect. Only ten days later the King had signed the Act. Strafford released Charles from his promise and Bishop Williams of Lincoln temporarily convinced him that his conscience as a King could override his conscience as an individual. The safety of the State demanded Strafford's execution. It was thought that fear for the safety of the Queen and their children played a part in the weakening of Charles's resolve, for there could be no telling what the mob would do if Strafford were reprieved.

Charles never forgave himself for his betrayal of his faithful adviser, and declared that his own execution was God's punishment for this crime. Laud's judgment, written in his diary on the day of Strafford's execution, was that Charles was a prince who 'knew not how to be, or to be made great'. Mr Wingfield-Stratford, in the second volume of his biography of Charles, *King Charles and King Pym,* has waxed indignant at the blatant chicanery of the charge that Strafford had committed treason. In legal terms this is no doubt correct. But the case for the opposition was well put long ago by Macaulay: Strafford's execution, he wrote, was justified not in legal terms but as a political act, as the slaughter of warfare was justified for the good of the whole community. 'The attainder was a revolutionary measure. It was part of a system of resistance which oppression had rendered necessary.'

ABOVE Seventeenth-century white satin panel, embroidered with figures of a king and queen and their attendants, chiefly in stump work.

RIGHT Needlework miniature of Charles I, from the mid-seventeenth century.

The logical result of Strafford's execution was that Charles should accept the permanent diminution of his power, and cooperate with the majority in Parliament. For a while, in the early summer of 1641, he seemed to accept such a situation and he gave his assent to a whole series of bills that fundamentally altered the relations between Crown and Parliament. The one most destructive of his own political power was the bill presented at the same time as the Attainder against Strafford, which forbade dissolution of the present Parliament without its own consent. The preamble to this bill justified it on purely technical grounds. Parliament was itself seeking to raise a loan to pay the Scots, and if Parliament were dissolved its creditors would have no resource. But it seems likely that so shrewd a tactician as Pym saw the political advantages to be gained by the measure. It was followed by a series of acts passed in June, July and August, which outlawed the various procedures used during the period of personal rule. The Tonnage and Poundage Act made collection of customs duties without Parliamentary grant illegal, as was any extension of the royal forests. The 'vexatious proceedings touching the order of knighthood' made it illegal to compel anyone to be knighted or to pay a fine. The prerogative courts, notably the Star Chamber and the court of High Commission, were abolished.

Although Charles gave his assent to all those bills, he did not genuinely accept this Parliamentary triumph as a permanent solution. There was talk again at the end of July of the principal leaders of Parliament being brought into office but nothing came of it. Instead the King departed at the beginning of August to Scotland, to the excitement and dismay of his opponents in Parliament and in London. They were so worried that they sent a committee, including Hampden, after him to see what he was engaged in; they also prepared to take the first steps towards setting up a military force under their own control. In fact, Charles, as usual, was only harming his own cause. He made no provision for carrying on the government in London while he was away, so that the initiative there passed even more into the hands of his opponents. Nor did he accomplish anything in Scotland. It was transparent that what he hoped for was some settlement of Scottish affairs that would allow him to use the Scottish army against his opponents in England. Given the

Archibald Campbell, 8th Earl of Argyll, defender of the liberties and religion of of Scotland: 'It was in Scotland ... that the torch was lighted which began the vast conflagration.'

natural affinity between the Presbyterian party in Scotland and the Parliamentary party in England, this was unlikely, but not altogether impossible. Personal intrigue among a few great magnates meant more in Scottish politics than it did in England, and it was not inconceivable that the Earl of Argyll, leader of the Covenanters, might be ousted in favour of the Marquis of Hamilton, who was more favourable to Charles's cause. Charles's efforts to win over some of the Scottish nobles at the expense of others failed disastrously. Any chance that he had of winning their support was ruined by the discovery of an

obscure plot to kidnap Argyll. The upshot was that Charles remained almost without authority in Scotland, and with another plot to be held against him. Pym made good use of this as soon as Parliament reassembled in October.

OPPOSITE Charles I resting during the chase, by Van Dyck.

At this point, with Charles still away in Edinburgh, the last act of the drama which was to bring civil war to England for the first time since 1485, opened with the news of the Irish rebellion. The facts were bad enough, from the English point of view: thousands of Protestant colonists murdered and thousands more sent fleeing from their homes. But the extent of the massacre was greatly exaggerated in the telling, and the fact that this was a religious war, a rising of Catholic Irish against the Protestant settlers planted there mainly by Charles and his father, added to the hysterical atmosphere which was to bring men in the end over the brink to civil war. In a more precise way, the Irish rebellion raised the stakes in the game that was being played at Westminster. A powerful army would have to be raised to restore English rule in Ireland. Up to this point the English army had consisted mainly of the ineffectual levies, held in check by the Scots. But if a real army were raised it could be used, either before or after settling the Irish affair, in England itself. Neither side would trust the other with control of this army. The opposition in Parliament were afraid that Charles would at last have the military power to crush them. There could be no doubt that he would use it. On his side Charles insisted that the control of the armed forces of the State was one royal prerogative that he could not surrender; he would not give up control of the army, he said, even to his wife.

In this insistence he began to find support among the Parliamentary gentry for the first time since the calling of the Short Parliament of 1640. In the autumn of 1641 a moderate Royalist party began to emerge, led by men such as Lord Falkland, Edward Hyde and Sir John Colepeper who had supported most of the earlier measures restricting the power of the Crown. The division in the Commons emerged most clearly in the debates of November, leading to the passing of the Grand Remonstrance on 22 November, amid violent scenes, long after midnight, and by a margin of only eleven votes. An often-quoted story tells us that Oliver Cromwell remarked that if the motion had been defeated he would have sold all he had and

emigrated to America. The Grand Remonstrance, although in form an address to the King, was really a manifesto to the nation, listing Charles's misdeeds from the beginning of his reign and demanding that in future his ministers should be 'such as the Parliament may have cause to confide in'. Another clause called for a synod of English and foreign clergymen to discuss the reformation of the Church. This was a victory for the party

ueraigne

A woodcut showing Charles being received by the Lord Mayor of London on his return from Scotland in November 1641. Charles's expedition to Scotland to win the support of the Scottish nobles against his English opponents was a disastrous failure.

which for the past twelve months had been demanding the abolition of episcopacy.

But although the religious question did much to divide the Commons and stimulated the formation of a Royalist party, it was not religion alone that made men draw back. The constitutional implications of the Grand Remonstrance were equally revolutionary. Pym's demands that Parliament should have the right to veto the King's choice of ministers, and to control the armed forces, were clearly not based on ancient precedents, however much the past was misinterpreted. This was a revolutionary programme. Moderates were also concerned about the methods Pym was using to force through his programme: the London mobs were again being called on, and the city was scarcely controlled by any public authority. The outburst of political and religious pamphleteering that followed the relaxation of censorship was also very worrying to moderate and conservative-minded men. The very foundations of Church and State, of private property and the social hierarchy, seemed to be on the verge of being called in question. Such fears were to be justified after the end of the Civil War, in 1647 and 1648, when truly extreme doctrines were propounded by the Levellers, and might have been put into practice if they had not met in the person of Cromwell, in contrast to Charles, a statesman who knew how to crush opposition in the bud.

The King returned from Scotland only on 25 November, and did not play an active part in the formation of a moderate Royalist party. Indeed, although he was in contact with Edward Hyde, the future Earl of Clarendon, Falkland and Colepeper, and had promised that they would be consulted before he took any grave decision, he took the gravest decision of all, to impeach five members of the Commons, without their advice. The opening of a legal process of impeachment for treason foreshadowed a sanguinary settling of accounts between the two parties. Can Charles really have thought that there would be a majority in either Lords or Commons for such a procedure? Was this not from the first but a legal cloak cast over an appeal to naked force, as was revealed when the Lords refused to order the arrest of the five members and Charles descended on the House of Commons in person at the head of an armed force?

On 4 January, after spending several hours in discussion with the Queen, Charles decided to take the plunge. Everyone was aware that something was afoot. It was quite unnecessary for Henrietta Maria to reproach herself, as she did to the end of her days, with having ruined the *coup* by careless talk that was repeated to Pym. Charles's coach moved slowly through the crowds from Whitehall to Westminster, and there was plenty of time for word to reach the Commons that the King was

six
1 You ar to accuse thofe ~~figue~~ joynt lie & feueraltie
2 you ar to referue the power of making addittionall
3 When the Comitie for examination is a naming (wch you must prefs to be clofe & under tey of fecresie) if eather Effex, Warwick, Holland, Say, ~~████~~ Wharton, or Brooke be named, you must defyre that they may be spared because you ar to examine them as witneffes for me

Charles R

coming in person to arrest the five members he had impeached, Pym, Hampden, Haslerigg, Holles and Strode, all leading members of the opposition. They escaped by boat and went into safe hiding in the City of London. When Charles arrived at the door of St Stephen's Chapel, the home of the Commons, he ordered his guards to remain outside. He entered, followed by his nephew, the young Elector Palatine, and took possession of the Speaker's chair. Never before had a reigning monarch entered the Commons' chamber. He formally explained that he had come to arrest the five members as they had not been delivered to his Sergeant-at-Arms yesterday. Then, looking around, he muttered: 'I do not see any of them. I think I should know them.' He asked, 'Is Mr Pym here?' No reply. 'Mr Holles?' No reply. He then asked the Speaker, William Lenthall, to point them out to him. Lenthall fell on his knees and said: 'May it please your Majesty. I have neither eyes to see nor tongue to speak in this place but as this House is pleased to direct me, whose servant I am.'

In this dramatic way the transition of the Speaker from his role of the Crown's manager of the Commons, still evident in

Charles I's instructions to Sir Edward Herbert, Attorney General, for the impeachment of the five members on 3 January 1642.

The Crown and the City

Charles depended on a prosperous London to provide him with funds and he needed the goodwill of the City magistrates. At first, like his father James, he had been able to borrow from the City, but he went too far and his credit was destroyed. Causes of resentment were grants of monopolies and attacks on the City's chartered privileges. Discontent became part of a more general unrest among the people caused by trade depression and unemployment, and, as 1641 drew to a close, it became clear that there was little support for the King's policies in the City. The Parliamentary Puritans quickly took over the political initiative in City government and organised the City militia against the King.

BELOW Part of the 'piazza' at Covent Garden.

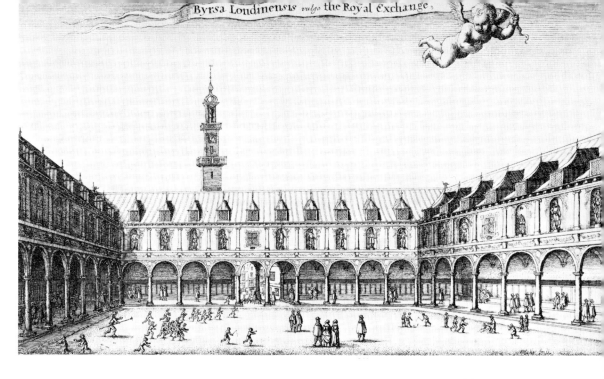

Byrsa Londinensis vulgo the Royal Exchange

THE
PROCTOR
AND
PARATOR
their Mourning:
OR,
The lamentation of the Doctors Commons
for their Downfall.

Being a true Dialogue,

Relating the fearfull abuses and exorbitancies of those
spirituall Courts, under the names of *Sponge*
the Proctor, and *Hunter* the Parator.

Printed in the yeare 1641.

ABOVE The Royal
Exchange in the
mid-seventeenth century
– hub of the City's
commercial life.
LEFT Satire on Laud's
spiritual courts which
attempted to check
religious dissent, and were
bitterly resented by the
citizens of London.
The receiver is shown
collecting fines from
religious transgressors.

123

1629 when he had been held in his chair to prevent him obeying the King's order to close the debate, to the servant of the Commons even against the King, was accomplished. Charles had no alternative but to look for himself. He did so, and remarked with a forced cheerfulness:

> Well, I see all the birds are flown, I do expect from you that you shall send them unto me as soon as they return hither. If not, I will seek them myself, for their treason is foul, and such a one as you will thank me to discover. But I assure you, on the word of a King, I never did intend any force, but shall proceed against them in a legal and fair way, for I never meant any other.

At that he walked back down the floor of the House and left, surrounded by his guards, while cries of 'Privilege' rose from the benches behind him. Charles's humiliation was not yet complete. The next day he went to the City to seek the missing men there. At the Guildhall he met the Common Council who refused to surrender them and instead demanded that he respect the privileges of Parliament. The same cry was heard in the streets as he drove back to Whitehall through hostile crowds. In the next few days it was made quite clear that no servant of the King would be able to arrest the five members in London; the City trained bands were called to arms to defend Parliament against the expected attack. It was no longer merely a mob of youths and apprentices, but solid respectable citizens who were in arms against the King under the command of Sergeant-Major Skippon. The royal guards were not strong enough to provide security even for the King and the royal family. Charles was overcome by his fear for the safety of Henrietta Maria, who, as a Catholic and because of her well-known intrigues with army officers and foreign powers, was hated by the opposition. On 10 January the royal family fled from London, sleeping that night at Hampton Court, where the King and Queen and their three eldest children had to share a bedroom. Charles was to return to London only as a prisoner after defeat in the Civil War; Henrietta Maria not until almost twenty years had elapsed. On the day that the royal family fled, Pym and his colleagues returned in triumph from the City to Westminster. The twelve-month duel between King Charles and King Pym had ended in victory for the latter. It remained to be seen whether armed force could reverse the verdict.

OPPOSITE Queen Henrietta Maria, by Van Dyck. This is one of a set of views of the Queen's head which were to assist Bernini in carving a marble bust of the Queen.

Great Rebellion
1642-8

ABOVE Charles I dictating despatches to Sir
Edward Walker, by an unknown artist.
BELOW Royalist soldiers from the windows of
Farndon Church, Cheshire. The windows were
built after the Restoration in 1660 in memory of
Cheshire gentlemen who fought for the King.

THE KING AND QUEEN moved from Hampton Court to Windsor, and then to Dover where Henrietta Maria with their younger children embarked for Holland, taking the Crown Jewels with her. Charles wished to be certain of his wife's safety before embarking on his attempt to reduce his rebellious subjects to obedience. They parted with many a sad embrace, and Charles followed the fleet that was carrying his beloved Queen away from him, riding along the cliffs, waving his hat in farewell. Before parting they had exchanged a code in which to correspond with each other in secrecy. When the ship put out to sea, Charles turned back, and with a small entourage made his way slowly north to York. No attempt was made to stop him, although he had only a small force at his disposal. Open hostilities had not yet commenced, and men were not likely to attempt to arrest the King.

His two eldest sons, the Prince of Wales (the future Charles II) and James, Duke of York, now nine years old, remained with the King. James was sent with a body of troops to the town of Hull, in the hope that his presence would encourage the governor to hand over the citadel to the King. Hull was a great prize, as it contained the stockpile of munitions that had been accumulated for the Scottish war, most of which had not been used. It would also be a most convenient point for communicating with Holland and Denmark. Charles's plans included one by which Henrietta Maria was to raise money by pawning the Crown Jewels, and then obtain a force of Danish mercenary soldiers for the King's army, but nothing came of this as she was unable to raise much money, and because the governor of Hull refused to open the gates of the city to the King. The failure of the King to secure any good port on the eastern and southern shores of England, and the fact that the navy went over to the side of Parliament, giving the opposition control of the seas, were to be two of the crucial elements in his defeat. The navy, for which he had incurred so much odium by the levying of ship money, was in no way grateful.

Meanwhile a war of manifestos began between the King at York, and Parliament in London. The King ordered loyal members of Parliament to leave London, so that the opposition now had undisputed control there. In June Edward Hyde left London, and joined the King at York. He was responsible for

PREVIOUS PAGES Early seventeenth-century musketeer loading and firing a heavy match-lock musket. He has a rest to support the gun and a bandoleer to carry his charges of powder.

129

the drafting of most of the King's declarations in answer to the manifestos which laid down the Parliamentary programme of reform. It was under Hyde's influence that the royal pronouncements provided a moderate and judicious theory of balanced government, in which both King and Parliament had their due share, a theory which was to have great influence for at least a century after the Restoration. They also helped at the time to reconstitute a Royalist party, which included many men who had opposed the King in 1640 and 1641. But the trouble was that it was very doubtful whether Charles really believed himself to be bound by these moderate declarations. Over the past two years his actions had often betrayed a different intention. Thus many took the other road, remaining on the side of Parliament, in spite of all their misgivings about the revolutionary implications of the Parliamentary programme for both Church and State. No doubt many sought, as long as possible, to remain uncommitted to either side, and pleaded for reconciliation when they could. But things had now gone too far for there to be reconciliation between King Charles and King Pym. By proclaiming that an 'ordinance' of the two Houses of Parliament had the force of law, the opposition had taken a clearly revolutionary step. By passing ordinances that placed military forces under their own control, the leaders of the opposition had gone beyond the point of no return. Unless they could defeat Charles in the field, he would be able to accuse them of high treason. When asked if he would grant Parliament's request to have control of the militia for a temporary period Charles replied: 'By God, not for an hour: you have asked that of me in this which was never asked of a King, and with which I will not trust my wife and children.'

In the summer of 1642 local skirmishes occurred in various parts of the country, and on 22 August the King made a formal call to arms, by raising the royal standard at Nottingham. It was not an auspicious occasion. Charles had made last minute alterations in the text of his proclamation which the herald found difficult to read. The blustery wind blew the standard down during the night. Although there were supporters of both parties in almost every county, the general position was that the north and west of England and Wales supported the King, while the south and east supported Parliament. This was already a

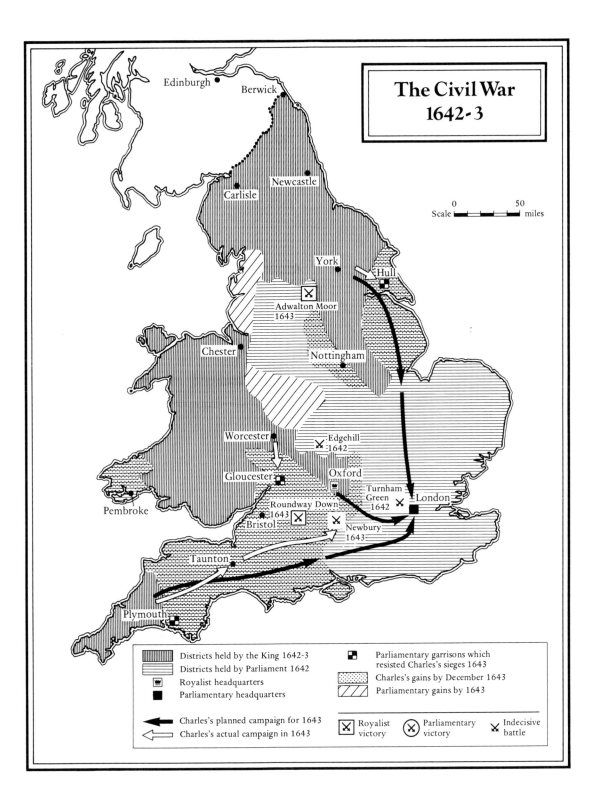

The Civil War
1642-3

Edinburgh
Berwick
Newcastle
Carlisle

Scale 0 ———— 50 miles

York
Hull

☒ Adwalton Moor
1643

Chester
Nottingham

Worcester
Edgehill
1642 ✗

Gloucester
Oxford ♔

Pembroke
Turnham
Green
1642 ✗ London

Roundway Down
1643 ☒
Bristol
Newbury
1643 ✗

Taunton

Plymouth

▥	Districts held by the King 1642-3	◼·␣ Parliamentary garrisons which resisted Charles's sieges 1643
▤	Districts held by Parliament 1642	⣿ Charles's gains by December 1643
♔	Royalist headquarters	⧄ Parliamentary gains by 1643
◼	Parliamentary headquarters	

➡ Charles's planned campaign for 1643
⇨ Charles's actual campaign in 1643

☒ Royalist victory   ⊗ Parliamentary victory   ✗ Indecisive battle

serious handicap to the royal cause. The King had the support of the poorer, less populated and less developed parts of the country, while Parliament had the more thickly-populated and prosperous areas. Money, as always, was one of Charles's chief concerns. In control of most of the ports, Parliament could levy customs duties, and it could borrow from the financiers of London. The King could only appeal to the loyalty of the gentry and aristocracy who had rallied to his cause, and then only so long as he controlled the areas where their estates lay, so that their rents continued to flow in. The melting down of the silver and gold plate of his supporters, and that of the Oxford colleges, would go a certain way to fill up his exchequer, but would certainly not be adequate for a long war.

In order to win, the King would have to strike quickly. He saw this, and made plans for an advance on London. His army was, no doubt, an *ad hoc* untrained force, but, officered by gentry whose education still involved swordsmanship and horsemanship, it might be expected to beat the 'tapsters and decayed serving men' who were thought to fill the ranks of the Parliamentary army. The first pitched battle of the Civil War, on 23 October 1642 at Edgehill, where the Cotswold hills dip down towards the Midland plain, was indecisive. The Parliamentary army was extricated and retreated to London, still a viable fighting force, but the Royalist advance was not checked. A month later, on 13 November, the advance guard of the King's army got as far as the village of Turnham Green, then a few miles outside London. After another indecisive skirmish, it drew back. Charles decided against taking the risk either of an assault in force on London, or of breaking through to Kent where he had much potential support. Hesitation at this moment probably lost him any chance he had of winning the war. He withdrew to winter quarters at Oxford, which was to be the seat of the Court for the rest of the war. Christopher Hibbert describes the scene in his book *Charles I*:

> By the beginning of the new year, 1643, Oxford was more like a garrison than a university town. Undergraduates, forsaking their books for spades, threw up new earthworks and fortifications; scholars and professors joined the colours; noble students sought leave to put on the gleaming armour of the King's Life Guard; soldiers were drilled in the streets and quadrangles; gunners were

The battle of Edgehill in October
1642, the first pitched battle of
the Civil War. The battle was
indecisive and the Parliamentary
army retreated to London.

The Court at Oxford

Having failed to enter London in the autumn of 1642, Charles withdrew with his army to Oxford, which became his headquarters and Court during the Civil War. The life of the Court continued as if its members were still at the Palace of Whitehall.

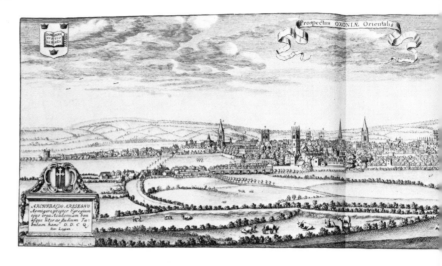

BELOW Silver crown of Charles I struck at Oxford (seen in miniature under the horse) in 1644.

RIGHT Royalist soldier, by William Dobson. A Royalist supporter, Dobson joined the Court in Oxford in 1642 where he painted many Royalists and the King's children.

134

ABOVE View of the city of
Oxford in the seventeenth
century.
RIGHT Abraham Bosse's
engraving of a cavalier in
the flamboyant dress of the
early 1640s.

135

trained in the meadows, and when off duty they brawled to such an extent that the sale of drink had to be prohibited after nine o'clock in the evening; duels were so commonplace that scarcely a day passed without an officer being wounded. . . .

At the same time the life of the Court went on as though its denizens were still in Whitehall. There were musical entertainments and plays; new sonnets and satires were published; new fashions were paraded through the streets and were copied by the citizens' wives; love affairs were conducted by the river bank and beneath the secluded walls of college gardens; fashionable ladies defied the 'terrible gigantique aspect' and 'sharp, grey eies' of the President of Trinity and walked into his chapel 'half dressed, like angels'; the King appointed a Master of Revels.

Charles himself maintained in public a characteristically wistful dignity. He took walks with Lord Falkland, now his secretary; he talked with his chaplains, with Jeremy Taylor, a Fellow of All Souls, and with Gilbert Sheldon, later to become Archbishop of Canterbury and Chancellor of the University; he attended the services in Christ Church with unfailing regularity; he contrived as best he could – though his own secret intrigues often conducted in direct contradiction of his public statements made him a less than successful mediator – to compose the quarrels which were for ever breaking out. . . .

The Royalist plan of campaign for 1643 involved a triple advance on London, from the north under the command of the Earl of Newcastle, from the west under Sir Ralph Hopton, and from Oxford. In spite of some successes at the battles of Adwalton Moor in Yorkshire and of Roundway Down in Wiltshire, the plan failed, as the Royalist advance slowed and hesitated. Parliamentary garrisons remained unreduced in both north and west, and the King's troops were reluctant to go far from their homes leaving them to the mercy of their enemies. The main Royalist force met the Parliamentary army under Essex at Newbury. Like Edgehill the previous year this was an indecisive battle, which ended with the King retiring to Oxford, and the Earl of Essex, commander of the Parliamentary army, retreating in good order towards London.

After a year's fighting the decisive success he needed still eluded Charles. In July 1643 he was re-united with the Queen at Oxford. Henrietta Maria had crossed the North Sea in terrible weather in January, landing near Bridlington in Yorkshire. She had spent the intervening months with the Royalist army in the north of England, and only in July did it become safe for her to join the King. That summer at Oxford there was a semblance of the old Court life, with the royal family quartered in colleges and University buildings. It was the last time that Charles was to enjoy the pleasures of civilian life with his Queen. The product of their reunion was to be another child, born at Exeter in May 1644, who was never to know her father (he saw her only once as a month-old baby) and was to grow to womanhood at her mother's exiled Court in France. By that time Henrietta Maria and Charles had parted for the last time. She made her way through disloyal Devon into the Royalist areas of Cornwall, and took ship from Falmouth to France. Her last pregnancy was a severe ordeal and this journey was a torture; she was ill before the birth and worse afterwards, and it took several months of recuperation at a small country house in the tranquil heart of France, far removed from the warfare and political conflicts of England, for her to regain her health.

'My youngest and prettiest daughter'

By the end of 1643 the royal armies were still disputing control of the north and south-west with the Parliamentary forces and any hope of a crushing co-ordinated advance on London had disappeared. In the long run this meant that the King had lost his chance to win the war. For a while it seemed that more could be hoped from diplomatic negotiations than from force of arms. In 1643 the Parliamentary side lost both Hampden and Pym, when the former was killed in battle and the latter died of natural causes. Pym's death, especially, was a blow. No one else could manage the House and its committees, and impose an overall political view as Pym had done. For a while all was con-fusion at Westminster. But before he died Pym had provided the machinery that was to win the war for Parliament. He had negotiated the Solemn League and Covenant with the Scots, who were to bring decisive military support at the battle of Marston Moor in 1644, and he had provided the fiscal resources that were used to pay a professional disciplined army. This he had done by the efficient organisation of local committees throughout the country to raise weekly sums, for which each county had been assessed by Parliament. He was also responsible for the Excise Ordinance, which imposed a purchase tax on certain common goods, such as wine, sugar, beer and linen.

The landing of Queen
Henrietta Maria near
Bridlington in Yorkshire
in July 1643, after
obtaining supplies on
the Continent for the
Royalist cause.

With these instruments and the development of Oliver Cromwell's military genius, victory for Parliament was assured in the long run.

In February 1644 there were negotiations between King and Parliament at Oxford, but no agreement could be reached. In effect, both sides demanded surrender by their opponents. Fighting was renewed in the spring, and Charles's armies moved out from Oxford in various directions. His sorties did not display much strategic purpose, but the fact that they were possible demonstrated that the Parliamentary side, through lack of organisation and the ineffectiveness of their generals, were still not utilising their superior military force in an effective way. Charles himself, bored with being confined in Oxford, went out with his troops and came under fire at the battle of Cropredy Bridge, near Banbury in June.

Only Prince Rupert, Charles's nephew and the hero of the Royalists, was fighting in the north in a way that could bring a decisive outcome. In his determination to win or lose he had Charles's support. Accordingly, having outmanœuvred his opponents who were besieging York, and relieved the city, he scorned to stay within the safety of the walls. Instead on 2 July 1644 he came out to meet the combined Parliamentary and Scottish armies at Marston Moor, in the largest pitched battle of the war. The rebels attacked at dusk, taking the Royalists by surprise; hours of hard fighting followed in which at times the Royalists seemed to have the upper hand. But the discipline and valour of Cromwell's cavalry, christened 'Ironsides' by Rupert after their day's work, brought victory to the other side. Rupert himself and six thousand cavalry escaped through the Yorkshire dales, back to Shropshire. But Marston Moor was the decisive battle of the war. The north of England was lost by the King and morale restored at Westminster. Decisive political changes were to bring more determined men to the front at Westminster, and to the command of the Parliamentary armies. The Earl of Manchester justified his cautious attitude by saying if they beat the King nine and ninety times, yet he was King still, while 'if the King beat us once, we shall be hanged'. Cromwell replied, indignantly: 'My lord, if this be so, why did we take arms at first? This is against fighting ever hereafter. If so, let us make peace be it never so base.' In essence, Cromwell's view pre-

OPPOSITE Prince Rupert of the Rhine, the son of Charles's sister Elizabeth of Bohemia, and a loyal supporter of King Charles. Although he was only twenty-three at the outset of the Civil War, he soon proved himself to be the ablest of the Royalist generals. In 1645 he was appointed General-in-Chief, but after the Royalist defeat at Naseby and the surrender of Bristol he lost his command.

Prince Rupert

141

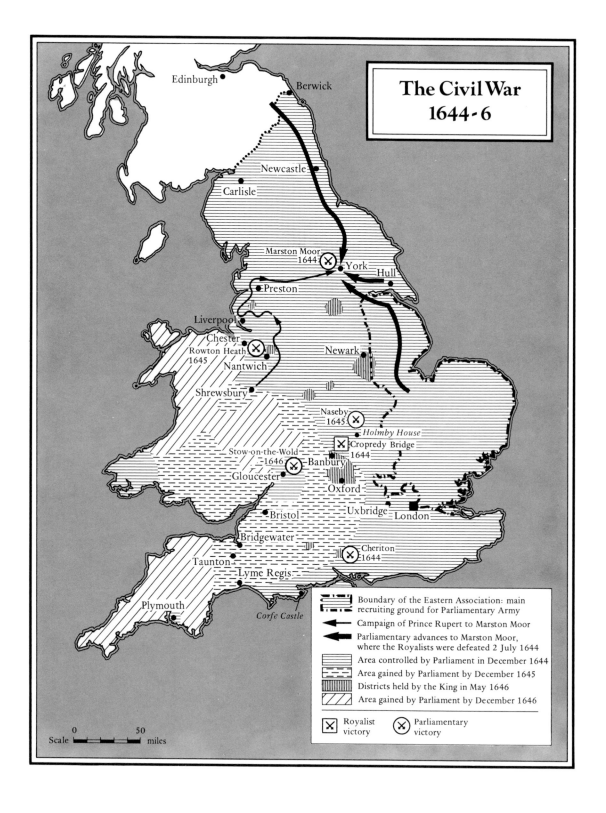

The Civil War
1644-6

Edinburgh
Berwick
Newcastle
Carlisle
Marston Moor
1644
York
Hull
Preston
Liverpool
Chester
Rowton Heath
1645
Nantwich
Newark
Shrewsbury
Naseby
1645
Holmby House
Stow-on-the-Wold
1646
Cropredy Bridge
1644
Banbury
Gloucester
Oxford
Bristol
Uxbridge
London
Bridgewater
Cheriton
1644
Taunton
Lyme Regis
Plymouth
Corfe Castle

Boundary of the Eastern Association: main
recruiting ground for Parliamentary Army
Campaign of Prince Rupert to Marston Moor
Parliamentary advances to Marston Moor,
where the Royalists were defeated 2 July 1644
Area controlled by Parliament in December 1644
Area gained by Parliament by December 1645
Districts held by the King in May 1646
Area gained by Parliament by December 1646

Royalist
victory

Parliamentary
victory

Scale 0   50   miles

vailed. The Self-Denying Ordinance, by obliging all members to resign their military commands, removed from control those whose caution had prevented them pushing home the victories of the Parliamentary armies. The creation of the New Model Army, a really professional, regularly paid force under the control of a single commander, was put in hand.

The winter's halt to campaigning allowed renewed negotiations between King and Parliament at Uxbridge. In spite of his military weakness Charles refused to make any real concessions. He was still hoping for overseas support to allow him to turn the tables on the rebels. He hoped that he would get money and arms from the Duke of Lorraine, an ambitious soldier with an unlimited capacity for making promises, and that a settlement of the conflict between Protestant and Catholic in Ireland would allow him to bring over an Irish army. This mirage danced before him for years without ever turning into reality. But his negotiations with the Irish, and the concessions he offered to the Catholics there, did him immense harm in England.

The New Model Army, commanded by Fairfax, with Cromwell as Lieutenant-General of Horse, finally destroyed Charles's hopes at the battle of Naseby in June 1645. Charles had been caught in the Midlands, unable to decide whether to push northwards in an attempt to join up with Montrose who was fighting for him in Scotland, or to move in the opposite direction, towards the south-west, where there were still areas under Royalist control. He divided his forces, sending some north and some to the south-west. This was a fatal mistake, and allowed Fairfax and Cromwell to strike an annihilating blow against the King's main army. The Royalist cavalry got away from the field, but the infantry and all the munitions were lost. The King still had scattered garrisons holding out all over the south-west and west of England, but he was unable to concentrate these forces into a new army. He did not join the largest body of troops that remained loyal to him in the south-west, but instead moved towards the Welsh border, and then spent nearly a year in aimless wandering with his personal bodyguard, during which the remaining Royalist forces were mopped up, one by one, by the enemy. In the end the King's movements became more and more those of a fugitive, until he returned to his stronghold of Oxford.

The opposing armies at the Battle of Naseby in 1645, an engraving by Joshua Sprigge in *Anglia Rediviva*. The King's defeat at Naseby finally destroyed all possibility of a Royalist victory.

145

Sr: beinge comanded by you to this
service, I thinke my selfe bound to ac=
quaint you with the good hand of God
towards you, and vs, Wee marched yesterday
after the Kinge whoe went before vs
from Dauentrie to Haurebrowe, and quar
tered about six miles from him, this day
wee marched towards him, Hee drew out
to meete vs, both Armies engaged, wee,
after 3. howres fight, very doubtfull
att last routed his Armie, killed and
tooke about 5000- very many officers

- -

I wish this action may begett thankfullnesse,
and humilitye in all that are conerxnred in itt,
Hee that ventres his life for tho libertye of
his cuntrie, I wish Hee trust God for the
libertye of his conscience, and you for the
libertye Hee fights for, In this Hee rests
whoe is
                    your most humble servant
Juno. 14th. 1645.   Oliver Cromwell
Haurebrowe.

The defeat at Naseby had been so complete that the King's papers had been captured. His opponents now knew all about his intrigues with the French and the Irish, his willingness to make concessions to the Papists in Ireland, while he had refused in January to accept the Presbyterian system in England. All this was soon published, adding to his reputation as a man who could not be trusted, and whose religious conscience was set harder against Presbyterianism than against Popery. In spite of the wreck of his military position, Charles still thought that he need not make too many concessions to his opponents. When Rupert told him that it was more prudent, 'to retain something than to lose all', he angrily declared: 'There is little question that a composition with them at this time is nothing less than a submission which . . . I am resolved against, whatever it cost me . . . Low as I am, I will not go less than what was offered in my name at Uxbridge.' On 11 January 1646, in reply to a letter from Henrietta Maria, in which she had pleaded with him not to jeopardise a chance of reaching agreement with the rebels for the sake of the episcopal organisation of the Church of England, Charles wrote:

> For the difference between me and the rebels concerning the Church is not a matter of form or ceremony, which are alterable according to occasion, but so real that if I should give way as is desired, here would be no Church, and no human probability ever to be recovered: so that, besides the obligation of mine oath, I know nothing to be an higher point of conscience.

Henrietta Maria, as a Catholic, could not see the religious importance of the difference between what from her point of view were only two different forms of heresy. But for Charles the maintenance of an episcopal form of Church government was essential on both religious and political grounds: on political grounds because it was vital for the maintenance of authority in society; on religious grounds because the apostolic succession, transmitted through the consecration of bishops from Jesus's disciples to the contemporary world, was the mark of a true Church.

The King's hopes, of course, lay in the well-known dissensions of his opponents. The Scots and the English were very far from seeing eye to eye and the Parliamentary side was by now

OPPOSITE Facsimile of a portion of the letter written by Cromwell to Lenthall, Speaker of the House of Commons, announcing the Parliamentarian victory at the Battle of Naseby.

The Parliamentarian Army

The early Parliamentarian troops were badly equipped, irregularly paid and ill-organised. Only the Eastern Association army, whose lieutenant-general Oliver Cromwell commanded the cavalry, was a disciplined and effective fighting force. Through Cromwell's efforts, the 'New Model Ordinance' of 1645 created a really professional fighting force – the New Model army – strong enough rapidly to crush the Royalists.

ABOVE The Earl of Essex, appointed the first Commander-in-Chief of the Parliamentary army in July 1642. After the defeat at Edgehill he remained nominally in command until 1645, but he had little power.

LEFT Carved wooden figures of soldiers of the New Model Army on the staircase of Cromwell House in London. On the left is an officer of pikemen, and on the right a musketeer.

RIGHT Sir Thomas Fairfax, who was created Commander-in-Chief of the New Model Army in 1645.

148

His
Excellencie
Sr Thomas Fairfax K
Generall of the forces
raised by the
Parliament.

Printed for John Partridg. Edw. Bower's Pinxit. W. Marshall Sculpsit.

149

deeply divided between Presbyterians and Independents, terms which covered political disagreements just as fundamental as the religious ones. When the Royalist Sir Jacob Astley surrendered to the Parliamentary troops in March 1646, he was only making the obvious comment when he said: 'You have done your work well boys. You may go play if you will not fall out amongst yourselves.' On 27 April 1646, Charles escaped from Oxford, which was now surrounded by Parliamentary forces. He had not yet told even his closest companions that he intended to seek out the Scottish army, but talked of escaping abroad, to France, to Ireland, to Denmark. But these were scarcely practical possibilities and he had probably already decided on his course of action, that of placing himself in the hands of his Scottish opponents. He was prepared to take the risk to his person, in the hope that negotiation with his enemies provided the best chance for the preservation of the monarchy. Before surrendering to the Scots he left these instructions to the Queen:

> I conjure you, by your unspotted faithfulness, by all that you love, by all that is good, that no threatenings, no apprehensions of danger to my person, make you stir one jot from any foundation in relation to that authority which the Prince of Wales is born to. I have already cast up what I am like to suffer, which I shall meet (with the grace of God) with that constancy that befits me. Only I desire that consolation, that assurance from you, as I may justly hope that my cause may not end with my misfortunes, by assuring you that misplaced pity to me do not prejudice my son's rights.

But if he had considered the worst that might befall him, it did not mean that he thought death at the hands of his enemies likely. Things had not yet come to such a pass.

In surrendering to the Scots Charles sought to turn Scots and English into irreconcilable enemies. Although the English Parliament had declared in favour of Presbyterianism, as part of the bargain struck in 1643, there were great differences between Scottish Presbyterianism and the desires of the Presbyterian party in the English Parliament. It has been pointed out that in the politics of these years the words 'Presbyterian' and 'Independent' denoted political tendencies which were not at all clear-cut in their views on Church government. The former, in fact, were far more moderate in their opinions than their

OPPOSITE Oliver Cromwell, by Peter Lely. He was a brilliant general and leader of men; even so hostile a witness as Clarendon admitted that 'He must have had a wonderful understanding in the natures and humours of men, and as great a dexterity in applying them ... he attempted those things which no good man durst have ventured on; and achieved those in which none but a valiant and great man could have succeeded...'

151

Scottish counterparts who sought to impose the fanatical Calvinist creed on the whole machinery of Church and State. Thus the first possibility for royal diplomacy was to set his English and his Scottish subjects against each other. Another possibility was offered by the rise of the Independents in the English Parliament and in the Parliamentary army. As their name implies, these men wanted an ecclesiastical system in which each parish was independent, deciding on its own forms of worship, not controlled by either episcopal or Presbyterian discipline. The implications of Independency might be revolutionary in both political and religious fields. It went along with a greater readiness to accept religious toleration than existed among either Episcopalians or Presbyterians, although few even among the Independents envisaged a world of many different churches in which the individual was free to choose the brand of religion that suited him best. These years saw the growth of all sorts of fanatical and mystical religious sects, and also the emergence from under the wings of the sects of a more fully democratic political creed, that of the Levellers.

There was plenty of evidence that to take away religious discipline would be a dangerous step. But it would be a grave mistake to think that all Independents held such revolutionary doctrines, either in politics or in religion. The leaders of the Independent party in Parliament and in the army were rich and respectable citizens. An Independent religious system might mean little more than increased authority for the country gentleman who had the patronage of the living, appointing the parish priest. It did not necessarily mean increased freedom for the ordinary member of the congregation. Nevertheless these radical possibilities existed. The importance of the Independents, and the weakness of the Presbyterians came from the fact that in the course of the Civil War the rank and file of the army had become politically conscious, as was vividly revealed in the mutinies and debates of the years 1647 to 1649. The Presbyterian majority in Parliament proved unable to control the army they had raised to defeat the King, thus placing power in the hands of those who could exert authority over the army. Those who, like Cromwell, could command support in the army, and were also members of Parliament, were in a key position. But Charles for a long time thought that he would himself be able to

OPPOSITE The title page of a Leveller speech delivered to General Fairfax in 1649. The Levellers emerged as a political force after the Civil War; led by John Lilburne, with support drawn mainly from the army, they demanded the abolition of the monarchy and a truly representative Parliament.

THE
Declaration and Standard

Of the *Levellers* of *England*;
Delivered in a Speech to his Excellency the Lord Gen. *Fairfax*,
on *Friday* last at White-Hall, by Mr. *Everard*, a late Member of the
Army, and his Prophesie in reference there unto; shewing what will
befall the Nobility and Gentry of this Nation, by their submitting to
community; With their invitation and promise unto the people, and
their proceedings in *Windsor* Park, *Oatlands* Park, and severall other
places; also, the Examination and confession of the said Mr. *Everard*
before his Excellency, the manner of his deportment with his Hat on,
and his severall speeches and expressions, when he was commanded
to put it off. Together with a List of the severall Regiments of Horse
and Foot that have cast Lots to go for *Ireland*.

Imprinted at *London*, for *G. Laurenson*, Aprill 23. 1649.

The frontispiece of a
Royalist book describing
early events in the
Civil War.

mediate between the army and Parliament. Defeated in war, he might still be able to re-establish something of his royal power as a result of the dissensions among his enemies.

This was a real possibility. The Presbyterian party in the Commons, worried about the radical implications both religous and secular of the programme of the Independents, were eager for a settlement with the King. This might well not have ended the matter. The real question was whether the army could be disbanded. For Parliament dared not impose on a discontented country, that already felt that it had been bled white, the taxation required to give the army its arrears of pay. The troops were certainly not prepared to lay down their arms without pay, and meekly accept the imposition of a Presbyterian religious system that seemed to many of them just as intolerable as the old episcopal Church. But, on the other hand, many men were eager for a restoration of law and tradition. If King and Parliament could come to terms this would be a strong argument. Those who resisted would have to convince the world, and themselves first of all, that they had good reason for such a blatantly revolutionary step. Both the King and the conservative-minded Presbyterian majority in the Commons had strong motives for agreement. To both of them the alternative of a loosely organised Church, as advocated by the Independents, in which there was virtually no authority above the parish level to impose uniformity of belief and ceremonial, was anathema. The implication of such a system was anarchy, both religious and political. And yet they were unable to reach agreement. Charles would not surrender the episcopal principle and the Presbyterians of the Commons would not accept it.

The terms offered to the King by the English Parliament, when he was still in the hands of the Scots in June 1646, were that he should subscribe to the Covenant, and that the Church should be organised along Presbyterian lines. In addition he was to surrender control of the militia to Parliament for twenty years; other clauses enshrined the constitutional ascendancy that Parliament had seized in 1641 and 1642. Charles sought to prolong the debate, thinking that the more he spun it out, the more indispensible he would become as his enemies quarrelled with one another. As the negotiations continued he recovered from the despondency into which he had been plunged by the depressing experiences of the last twelve months, before he rode out from Oxford. He asked to be allowed to come to London. It was transparently obvious that he thought that he would be better placed there to intrigue with the different parties. Meanwhile he argued obstinately about points that many thought trifling, given the circumstances. The Scottish observer Robert Baillie wrote in his diary in May 1646: 'It has been the King's constant unhappiness to give nothing in time: all things have been given at last: but he has ever lost the thanks, and his gifts have been counted constrained and extorted.' In a letter to a friend Baillie declared: 'If that man now goe to tinckle on Bishops and delinquents, and such foolish toyes, it seems he is mad.'

In January 1647 the first of Charles's cards was trumped. Parliament reached agreement with the Scots, paying them over half a million pounds for their services to the common cause. The Scots went home, handing the King over to Parliamentary commissioners, and for a few months left the English to settle their own affairs. Charles was moved south to Holmby House, an enormous Tudor mansion in Northamptonshire. He was still treated formally with all the deference due to a King, although he was, of course, a prisoner under guard. But his journey appeared as almost a triumphant progress through a loyal country, so many people flocked to see the King and to pay their respects to him. This popularity, in contrast to the murmurings of the days before 1640, probably increased Charles's self-confidence. He did not fully realise that popularity in the country at large was a weak thing to place in the scales against the organised force of the army, and the political skills acquired in a hard school by the men with whom he had to deal. These men, of whom the most important were Cromwell and his son-in-law Henry Ireton, were playing a dangerous and difficult game. They had to take account of the situation in Scotland and in Ireland, of majority opinion in Parliament, and also of opinion among the army. One important issue for the rank and file of the army was the question of their arrears of pay. But this was not the only issue that engaged their attention. As was shown in the Putney debates, and on many other occasions between 1647 and 1649, there were strong, if inchoate, currents of opinion on political and religious matters in the army. One final piece on the political chessboard was the King himself, and the army leaders were keen to negotiate with him on their own account in 1647. So just as Charles saw one opportunity for playing off his enemies against each other disappear, as the Scots withdrew, another opportunity arose in the division between Presbyterians and Independents among the English.

Matters came to a head in June 1647 when Parliament sought to disband the army without making proper arrangements for arrears of pay. It was well known, also, that the Presbyterian majority in the Commons sought to impose Presbyterianism on the country. Charles had just agreed to a scheme that imposed Presbyterianism for three years, while a final settlement of Church affairs was prepared by an assembly of twenty divines. The rank and file of the army refused to disband and agreed to meet at Newmarket. 'The grandees', as the senior officers were called, joined them, including Cromwell and Ireton, and it was decided that the army would refuse to disband. The next day, 3 June, Cornet Joyce and a small band of soldiers arrived at Holmby House and took charge of the King. When Charles asked by what warrant he was being taken, Joyce pointed to the ranks of soldiers drawn up outside the house. Charles smilingly accepted the situation, saying that the warrant was written in as fair and legible a hand as he had seen. There can be little doubt that Joyce was acting on orders from Cromwell, who was determined to prevent an agreement being reached between the King and the Presbyterians in Parliament. The King was moved to various places, eventually reaching Hampton Court on 24 August.

He negotiated now with the army leaders, including Ireton, and was more confident than ever that he would be able to play off army against Parliament, so as to win back for himself a large part of the royal power. In fact the army leaders were determined not to allow Charles to mediate between them and Parliament. They were determined to fix the terms on which he could be restored to the throne, terms summarised in the Heads of the Proposals, drawn up by the army during the summer in 1647. This scheme, the most radical constitutional programme that ever had any serious chance of implementation, was far removed from anything that Charles had in mind. Encouraged

'It is written in characters fair and legible'

Hampton Court Palace, by Henry Danckerts, one of Charles's favourite palaces. He was confined there in August 1647 by Cromwell, but he was not closely guarded and in November he escaped to the Isle of Wight.

by a riot in London, when the cry of 'King and Covenant' was heard, Charles rejected the army's proposals. He thought that they needed the King more than he needed them, and that therefore they would have to produce a scheme more in keeping with his own ideas. In fact events were now moving rapidly to disprove Charles's assessment of the situation. The army was soon to demonstrate that it needed neither King nor Parliament. Both King and Parliament appealed to law and tradition, and for both it was a largely specious appeal, only a thin disguise for the emptiness of their claims. The army moved into London, restoring to Parliament about sixty Independent members who had fled to their friends in the army for protection during the brief rising, in the course of which the mob had invaded West-minster. Now some of the Presbyterian members fled in their turn. Authority in England was more and more that of the sword, although the process was not complete for another eighteen months when Colonel Pride purged the Commons as a preliminary to the trial and execution of the King.

Nevertheless, in the autumn of 1647 the army leaders were still reluctant to expose the realities of their power. The Presbyterian party in Parliament were allowed once again to submit their scheme to the King, by which he would be restored as the

puppet King of a Presbyterian country. Charles told them that he preferred the army's radical document, the Heads of the Proposals. He was revelling in the opportunity to play off one faction against another, and thinking again of a deal with the Scots that might restore him to the throne on better terms. If nothing came of that he seemed to think that peerages for the army leaders, 'the grandees', might work wonders and lead them to agree to a restoration on better terms than the Presbyterians offered. Cromwell and Ireton still wanted a settlement with the King, but they were well aware of the pressure from the rank and file of the army for a political and religious revolution that went far beyond anything Charles dreamed of. In the autumn of 1647 some remarkably democratic proposals were being aired. 'The Agreement of the People', sponsored by the army Levellers, demanded the abolition of the monarchy, and a truly representative Parliament. Such radical schemes were discussed at Putney in October and November by representatives of the regiments and by the army leaders. Cromwell and Ireton knew the strength of the pressure from below in a way that the King never did. One of the Leveller demands in these debates was that there should be no more negotiations with the King.

Charles imprisoned in Carisbrooke Castle on the Isle of Wight, where he was held from November 1647 to December 1648, from a contemporary broadsheet. Charles's intrigues from Carisbrooke stirred up Royalist risings in several parts of the country; these were quickly suppressed, but they made Charles's execution inevitable.

Meanwhile Charles was seeking to escape from captivity so as to have full freedom to negotiate with all the factions. At the end of October he settled the terms with the Scots by which they agreed to help him. He had given his word of honour not to escape, but he managed to square his conscience to his own satisfaction, and on 11 November he rode away from Hampton Court. He had not been closely guarded and it has even been suggested that Cromwell connived at his escape. One of the mysteries in the affair is that he chose to go to the Isle of Wight, and to surrender himself to its governor, Robert Hammond, a relative of Hampden and a friend of Cromwell. But Charles seems to have thought that Hammond would be sympathetic, and that, at the worst, it would be easy to escape from the Isle of Wight to the Continent. In fact he soon became a prisoner more closely guarded at Carisbrooke Castle than he had been at Hampton Court. From Carisbrooke Charles sent further proposals to Parliament, granting Presbyterianism for three years, and limited religious toleration, and giving up control of the militia for the rest of his reign. Parliament replied with counter propositions. At this point Cromwell and Ireton, who had previously tried to reach an agreement with the King, changed into determined opponents. They were suspicious of his dealings with the Scots and it was becoming steadily more obvious that a settlement with the King would provoke an explosion in the army where Leveller sentiment was as strong as ever. Their suspicions of his intrigues in Scotland were justified by the agreement made in December, when the Scots promised to invade England to restore Charles to the throne and Presbyterianism was guaranteed for three years.

Charles's activities had now so stirred up the embers that civil war blazed up again for a few brief months. There were army mutinies, apprentice riots in London, and then, in May, the first of a series of Royalist risings. The Royalist risings in widely scattered parts of the country, in Wales, in Kent, in Essex and throughout the north, were scarcely co-ordinated and were easily dealt with by the army. It has been said that they were more the result of economic distress and the general discontent with Parliamentary and military rule, than the product of positive enthusiasm for Charles's cause. The only serious danger came from the Scots. The Scottish invasion, however, was postponed until July because of political disputes in Scotland, and when it came the Scottish army was a weak and untrained force. By the time the Scots reached Preston in August, Cromwell had had time to settle the rising in South Wales and to move northwards to win one of his most decisive victories. He went on to invade Scotland and to overturn the balance of political forces there, replacing Hamilton who had come out for Charles with the anti-Royalist Argyll. But he did not make a clean sweep, thus allowing the Scots one more attempt to interfere in English affairs two years later.

Charles made desperate efforts to escape from the Isle of Wight so that he could join the Scots or one of the English risings. But he was too closely guarded and he had to watch the defeat of all his hopes in impotent inactivity at Carisbrooke. The Second Civil War sealed Charles's fate. There was a stronger demand than ever from the rank and file of the army for the punishment of Charles Stuart, 'that man of blood'. Cromwell and Ireton had no desire to begin another round of negotiations with so unsatisfactory an interlocutor. If the more radical demands of the Levellers were to be diverted, the trial and execution of the King would be a useful lightning conductor. Thus, although Charles was allowed to spend the autumn months in more prolonged negotiations of the sort that had filled his life since 1646, they came to take on an air of increasing unreality. The King and the Parliamentary commissioners, meeting in the little town hall of Newport on the Isle of Wight, argued endlessly back and forth about the same old problems of the government of the Church and the control of the armed forces. But it became daily more evident that neither King nor Parliament could hope to command the armed forces at all, and that the same armed forces were determined not to allow either the King to re-establish episcopacy or the Parliament to establish Presbyterianism.

'We will cut off the King's head with the crown on it'

7 The King Condemned 1649

CHARLES'S TRIAL and execution were the supreme moment of his life, and one of the great dramatic incidents of English history. No longer trying, as he had done so frequently and so unsuccessfully, to play the role of Machiavellian politician, he could, as he said, if unable to live like a King, die like a gentleman. He had never lacked courage; now he was borne up by the certainties of his religious faith, and by his conviction that his own death would serve the royal cause better than any other solution. At no time after the defeat of his armies at Naseby had he given serious consideration to escaping to the Continent. Instead, he had stayed to act out his role among his rebellious subjects to the bitter end. The continuity of the royal line was not in doubt, as the Prince of Wales was safe overseas and would soon be old enough to play a man's role in the world. His one concern was lest the enemies of the royal House should be able to divide his family. At his last meeting with two of his youngest children, who had been left behind in the precipitate flight of 1642 and had been prisoners of the rebels ever since, he attempted to impress on them the necessity of loyalty to their elder brother, soon to be the head of the family and of the State. To the Princess Elizabeth, aged thirteen, he spoke of the need whenever she should have the opportunity, to impress on her brother James the duty that he owed to his elder brother. To Henry, aged eight, he insisted in simple and direct language, suitable to the boy's years: 'They will cut off my head, and perhaps make thee a King: but mark what I say, you must not be King so long as your brothers Charles and James do live.' The child replied: 'I will be torn in pieces first.' This was on 29 January 1649, when his custodians allowed the children to be brought up from Syon House to say a last farewell to their father.

Charles believed that the enormity of his execution would lead to a revulsion of feeling in favour of the Crown and thus to a restoration of the monarchy. In this expectation he was not wrong, except as to the time-scale involved. It was not to be an immediate result, but one that took eleven years and many lucky chances. But Charles was firmly convinced not only of the righteousness but of the inevitable triumph of his cause. Just as much as Cromwell and the Calvinists, he believed that everything that happened in the world was a sign of God's favour or

Prince Henry and Princess
Elizabeth, by Peter Lely.
Charles said a last farewell
to the two children the day
before his execution. He
impressed upon them the
need to support their eldest
brother and the legal
descent of the Crown.

One of the last portraits of Charles I with his second son James, Duke of York, by Peter Lely.

disfavour. The disasters that had befallen him and his country, were by the will of God, who would not turn His face aside forever. God was punishing him for the great sin of his life, his signature to the unjust Act for the execution of his faithful servant Strafford. But God would not forever withhold His favour from the people of England. In the end, and perhaps quite soon, the restoration of the monarchy would come. If his own execution led to that result it was far better than some patched up compromise that left him a king in name only, a puppet in the hands of the leaders of the erstwhile Parliamentary army. He wrote to the Prince of Wales in late November 1648:

> The English nation are a sober people: however at present under some infatuation. We know not but this may be the last time we may speak to you or the world publicly. We are sensible into what

hands we are fallen: and yet, we bless God, we have those inward refreshments the malice of our enemies cannot perturb; we have learned to busy ourself in retiring into ourself, and therefore can the better digest what befalls, not doubting but what God's Providence will restrain our enemies' malice and turn their fierceness to his praise. To conclude, if God give you success, use it humbly and far from revenge. If He restore you to your right upon hard conditions, whatever you promise, keep. . . . We do not more affectionately pray for you (to whom we are a natural parent) than we do that the ancient glory and renown of this nation be not buried in irreligion and fanatic humour: and that all our subjects (to whom we are a political parent) may have sober thoughts as to seek their peace in the orthodox profession of the Christian religion as it was established since the Reformation in this kingdom, and not in new revelation; and that the ancient laws, with the interpretation according to the known practices, may once again be a hedge about them: that you may in due time govern and they be governed, as in the fear of the Lord.

What he meant by saying that he might not be able to speak again publicly was that he might be murdered in some secret fashion. But his enemies had not the least intention of that. Rather they were to play into his hands by providing him with a stage in the form of a public trial and execution. From the moment that Charles's plotting had brought about the Second Civil War in 1648, it was likely that he would be brought to public trial and execution. His opponents were far too sure of their own righteousness to want to despatch him in a hole-and-corner way. Even before setting off to meet the Scots and the other Royalist armies in the summer of 1648, a strong party among the army officers had determined 'to call Charles Stuart, that man of blood, to an account for that blood he had shed and mischief he had done, to his utmost, against the Lord's cause and people in these poor nations'.

It was this that gave universal significance to Charles's death. Kings had been deposed and murdered before, in England as in other countries. This time, as Cromwell put it, 'we will cut his head off with the crown on it'. From this moment a new principle had entered the political life and thought of Western Europe, expressed in the claim of the 'Rump' of the Long Parliament, on 4 January 1649, that 'the people were under God the source of all just power'. Charles had an easy task in pointing

OPPOSITE Charles I
cutting down the tree of
religion from a Puritan
satire. Only the final
elimination of Charles
could lead to the reform of
the Church of England
which the powerful
Puritan party in the
Army demanded.

out that the power that tried him was that of a minority resting
on the sword, but the principle had been asserted, and was to be
broadened out in eighteenth-century liberal thought, and in the
American and French Revolutions. Against this principle,
Charles asserted the old idea of monarchical power as a trust
from God: 'a subject and a sovereign are clean different things'.
This clash of ideologies made the trial and execution a truly
tragic moment in history, in which two great ideals were
asserted. As always, the ideals were embodied in human vessels
that had the normal share of weakness. Charles had certainly
revealed many faults in his career as a ruler; those who regarded
him as responsible for the loss of so many lives were not altogether wrong: he *was* responsible, although others were also.
But in January 1649, personally helpless in the hands of his
enemies and obviously about to die, Charles was a noble figure,
and able to embody his ideal in a way that added an entirely new
mystical element to High Tory royalism and Anglicism. There
was no other individual in the courtroom who could match
him. The only man who could have done so, Cromwell,
remained behind the scenes, although it was his driving will that
impelled the matter to a conclusion.

The stage was set in the autumn of 1648 while Charles was
engaged in more of his wordy disputations with the Parliamentary commissioners at Newport on the Isle of Wight. As always,
he thought that time was on his side, when it certainly was not,
and he argued endlessly about details, 'Until Cromwell had
done his work in the north and marched up to Towne to make
the Treaty ineffectual' as Clement Walker put it in his polemical
History of Independency. Resumption of warfare in the summer
of 1648 had shifted the balance of power in the Commons back
to the Presbyterian side and away from the Independents. But
this was a temporary and unreal situation, the result of the
absence of leading Independent members, like Cromwell,
recalled to service in the army. In a slightly longer perspective
the resumption of warfare could only strengthen the army and
its sympathisers against the civilian element in the Commons.
Parliament had long ceased to be the sole arbiter of the situation.
Even if Charles and the Parliamentary commissioners had come
to terms, it is not very likely that they could have been imposed
on the army and on other radical groups, such as the citizens of

John Lilburne, the volatile leader of the Levellers, whose ideas of political freedom and reform were far more extreme than those of Cromwell and the Army leaders.

London who petitioned Parliament in September against a treaty with the King, demanding something akin to the Leveller programme. Charles's prolonged talks with the Presbyterian leaders of the Commons only convinced the army leaders that drastic action was needed.

Cromwell played a curiously inactive role at this time, as he not infrequently did, remaining at the unimportant siege of the last Royalist stronghold at Pontefract. His son-in-law, Henry Ireton, however, was at the centre of some feverish political activity. A group of army officers was demanding that Charles be brought to justice. Others, even more radical, with an un-determinable amount of support among the rank and file in the army and also among civilians 'of the meaner sort', wanted the trial of the King to be only one element in a total political and social revolution. Ireton engaged in debate with these radicals, Lilburne, Wildman and other Levellers, and saw the need for

Henry Ireton, an able soldier and politician and staunch supporter of Cromwell, who became his father-in-law in 1646. He had little sympathy with the unpractical schemes of the Levellers, and tried to arrange a settlement with the King until Charles's behaviour on the Isle of Wight convinced him that this was impossible.

some dramatic gesture to divert attention from dangerous talk that might lead to the upsetting of property rights.

This was the background to the events of the first week in December 1648, when the army returned in force to London, having done its work of crushing the Royalists. On 1 December Charles was moved from Carisbrooke Castle to much closer and less pleasant imprisonment at Hurst Castle, situated on a spit of land jutting out into the Solent, surrounded on all sides by water. There could be no hope of escape from such a spot. On 4 December the House of Commons declared that the King had been removed without its consent and at the end of an all-night sitting voted to resume negotiations with him. The next day, 6 December, Colonel Pride arrived at the House before the sitting began and, with the help of Ireton, turned away or arrested all members who were out of sympathy with the army as they arrived. After 'Pride's Purge', those who ruled the army

The Rump and dreggs of the house of Com remaining after the good members were purged out.

Playing card attacking the Rump Parliament, which remained after Colonel Pride in 1648 had expelled from Parliament all the Members who were out of sympathy with the army. The Rump was finally dissolved by Cromwell in April 1653.

could do what they wanted with Parliament; many besides those excluded decided that it would be wise not to attend, and only those members most in sympathy with the army leaders remained in attendance at what was derisively known as the Rump. Only after this did Cromwell arrive back in London, and announce his agreement with the steps taken. It may be that he would have managed things differently had he returned earlier, engineering a purge by majority vote of the Commons, a less blatant assertion of military power, but the deed was done and he endorsed it. His strong personality was the driving force behind the subsequent developments that brought Charles to trial in Westminster Hall and to the scaffold in Whitehall.

Charles seized this opportunity as he had no other in the course of his whole reign. There can be no doubt that the events of January 1649 made much better propaganda for the Royalist than for the Republican cause, largely because of the mismanagement of the affair by his enemies. There was a case to be made against Charles, but it was made in the worst possible way, as a result of the procedures adopted by Charles's opponents. Although the step they had taken was revolutionary in the extreme, they attempted to couch it in the traditional legal terminology. This placed all the cards in Charles's hands. By refusing to plead, he made it impossible for the court to bring forward the witnesses they had provided to make their case against him. They were brought before a committee of the court, and their depositions read out in public session on 25 January, but this did not have the same effect. The most dramatic part of the court proceedings consisted of Charles's various clashes with the President, in the course of which he was able to make a skilful and eloquent presentation of his case.

In readiness for the trial Charles was taken from Hurst Castle by way of Winchester, where he was ceremonially received by the mayor and aldermen, and through Farnham, to Windsor Castle. The arrangements for his journey had been made by Colonel Harrison, the officer who had first accused him as 'that man of blood', and Charles had some conversation with him at Farnham. Harrison assured him that there was no question of a plot to murder him: what was to be done 'would be open to the eyes of the world'. At Windsor Castle Charles was reduced completely to the state of a prisoner. His servants were only six

in number and one officer was to be with him at all times. No
longer was there any pretence that he was to be revered as His
Royal Majesty. Down to that time some symbolic relics of the
old Court rituals had been preserved, even in the close confinement of Hurst Castle. The royal dinner had even there been
served on bended knee, with all the ritual of the uncovering and
tasting of dishes (to guard against poison) and the admission
of such of the public as came to see the spectacle. Now Charles
dined and supped privately and without ceremony. On 19
January 1649 he was brought into London and lodged at St
James's Palace.

176

The time since the New Year had been taken up with making ready Westminster Hall, with setting up the High Court of Justice, and the framing of the charge in due legal terms, which did not prove easy. One hundred and thirty-five names were chosen to make up the Commissioners of the High Court. There was an attempt to make the list the most respectable that could be obtained, and it included landowners from all over the country and citizens of the main towns. Many were members of Parliament, others prominent army officers. The list began with Fairfax, still nominally supreme commander of the army, although he had relapsed into complete passivity. He did not

Hollar's etching of Westminster Hall in the mid-seventeenth century, where the trial of Charles I took place.

177

withdraw his name, although he never attended the meetings of the court, and at the opening session when his name was called out, a masked lady, in fact Lady Fairfax, shouted out 'No, nor will he be here: he has more wit than to be here.' The lawyers were even more cautious, and the two chief justices, Henry Rolle and Oliver St John, and John Wilde, Chief Baron of the Exchequer, although all opponents of the King, refused to allow their names to figure. Others who were not at the centre of things were not asked whether they were willing to serve: their names were merely published as commissioners. But nothing was done actually to compel attendance, although, no doubt, pressure was brought to bear on those who could be reached. In the end there were always at least sixty-seven commissioners present, and fifty-nine of them signed the judgment, with its sentence of death.

The trial took place in Westminster Hall, that magnificent medieval building which had for centuries been the hub of English justice. As the great hall was for normal purposes divided up by wooden partitions into different courts, a good deal of preparation was required to make it suitable for a great show trial. Arrangements also had to be made to provide security. In fact no attempt was made to rescue the King or to assassinate his judges, but it was as well to be sure. John Bradshaw, the president of the court, had a special metal protective lining put in his hat, and things were arranged so that the seats for the general public were well away from the prisoner and the commissioners, who were protected by guards. The ordinary spectator, in fact, had little chance of seeing or hearing what was going on, but proceedings were reported by the writers of the various news-sheets that had sprung up during the Civil War. The trial was a well publicised event.

On 20 January Charles was brought down the Thames by boat and led into the hall, carefully guarded by the soldiers. Apart from the formal announcement that he was to be tried, he had been given no information and he knew nothing about the form and composition of the court, or about the nature of the charge. But his line of action was clear and never in doubt: it was to deny the competence of any court to try the King. The charge was read out by John Cook, the lawyer who had accepted the task of making the case against Charles. It began by stating that the King had been 'trusted with a limited power to govern by, and according to the laws of the land, and not otherwise'. But he had attempted 'to erect and uphold in himself an unlimited and tyrannical power', and had 'traitorously and maliciously levied war against the present Parliament and the people therein represented'. He had sought foreign support for this enterprise, and had 'caused to be renewed the said war against the Parliament and good people of this nation in this present year'. Therefore he was responsible for 'all the treasons, murders, ravages, burnings, spoils, desolations, damages and mischiefs to this nation, acted and committed in the said wars'. Cook concluded that he therefore impeached 'the said Charles Stuart, as a Tyrant, Traitor and Murderer, and a public and implacable Enemy to the Commonwealth of England'. At these words Charles laughed scornfully.

The President now asked Charles what answer he made to the charge. He had never been prompt of speech and had preferred in other days to have his speeches and declarations prepared for him by his advisers. At that time he had said that he was a better cobbler than he was a shoemaker, and he preferred to have a draft presented to him in which he would make corrections and amendments. Now he was alone, without advisers, except for Juxon, the Bishop of London, who had been allowed to share his captivity to provide spiritual consolation. He was not, of course, present in the courtroom, and Charles had to frame his own answer. He did so cogently and eloquently, and without trace – at least no mention is made of it in any of the accounts of the trial – of his customary stammer. He began: 'I would know by what power I am called hither. I would know by what authority – I mean lawful. There are many unlawful authorities in the world, thieves and robbers by the highway. . . . Remember I am your King, your lawful King, and what sins you bring upon your heads, and the judgment of God on this land. . . .' After several bitter exchanges with the president of the court, Charles was ordered to be removed, and the court was adjourned until Monday, the next day being Sunday.

During the week-end Charles had time to clarify his ideas by making a brief written exposition of his reasons for refusing to accept the authority of the Court. He began by restating his claim that 'No earthly power can justly call me (who am your

'Remember I am your King'

179

The King on Trial

On 20 January 1649, Charles was brought to trial on the charge of high treason and was impeached 'as a Tyrant, Traitor and Murderer, and a public and implacable Enemy to the Commonwealth of England'. The trial was one of the few great moments of Charles's life: he defended himself with dignity and courage, challenging the right of the court to try their King.

ABOVE The hat, with a with a special metal protective lining, worn by Bradshaw during the trial. RIGHT The chair in which Charles sat during the trial.

180

LEFT John Bradshaw (left) the president of the court which tried Charles, and Hugh Peters (right) one of the small group of determined men who drove the trial through. Peters was executed for High Treason at the Restoration; Bradshaw died peacefully in 1659.

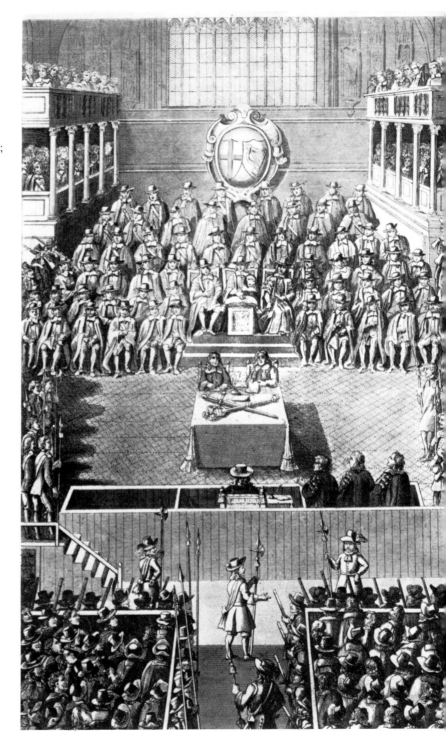

RIGHT A contemporary engraving of the trial in Westminster Hall.

*'The duty
I owe to God...
will not suffer me
to be silent'*

King) in question as a delinquent.' He said that if he alone were concerned he could be content with that overwhelming argument, 'But the duty I owe to God in the preservation of the true liberty of my people will not suffer me to be silent. For how can any free-born subject of England call life or anything he possesseth his own, if power without right daily make new and abrogate the old fundamental laws of the land?' Therefore he would state the other reasons that made the supposed Court incompetent to try not only the King, 'but the meanest man in England'. His first principle was that:

> There is no proceeding just against any man, but what is warranted either by God's laws, or the municipal [i.e. national] laws of the country where he lives. Now I am most confident this day's proceeding cannot be warranted by God's laws. For, on the contrary, the authority of obedience unto Kings is clearly warranted, and strictly commanded in both Old and New Testament, which if denied, I am ready instantly to prove.

He then showed that it was equally impossible to justify the trial by any particular English law. Was it not a lawyer's maxim that the King can do no wrong? In any case the House of Commons alone was not itself a court and could certainly not erect a court by its own authority. 'And it were full as strange that they should pretend to make laws without the King or Lords' House, to any that have heard speak of the laws of England.' Even, he went on, if it were admitted that the people could authorise such a departure from old and known laws,

> I see nothing you can show for that, for certainly you never asked the question of the tenth man in the Kingdom, and in this way you manifestly wrong even the poorest ploughman, if you demand not his free consent. . . . Thus you see that I speak not for my own right alone, as I am your King, but also for the true liberty of all my subjects, which consists not in the power of government, but in living under such laws, such a government as may give themselves the best assurance of their lives, and property of their goods.

Finally, he made the obvious point that those who had claimed to speak in the name of the people of England were not even a proper House of Commons, for 'it is too well known that the major part of them are detained or deterred from sitting'.

He began to present these arguments to the court at the next session on 22 January, but was not allowed to proceed very far before he was interrupted by Bradshaw. After prolonged argument Charles was again ordered to be removed from the court. The next day the same arguments about the incompetence of the court were resumed and ended as before with the order for Charles's removal. To Bradshaw's final declaration that 'You are, notwithstanding you will not understand it, to find you are before a court of justice', Charles replied 'I see I am before a power.' The proceedings had so far achieved nothing beyond allowing the King to advertise the illegality of the court, and the fact that the remnants of his Parliamentary opponents were totally dependent on the army leadership. Charles's own arbitrary acts in the days before 1640 were trivial in comparison with the present domination of the land by military force. The court decided in the end to sit as a committee to hear the evidence against Charles which could not be presented formally as he refused to plead. This occupied the next two days, and on 26 January the court assembled, without the King, to decide on the sentence: that the King 'be put to death by the severing of his head from his body'.

The next day, 27 January, Charles was brought before the court, and again asked if he wanted to speak in his own defence before sentence was passed. He asked to be allowed to speak before the Lords and Commons. Bradshaw was about to deny this when Downes, one of the commissioners, protested, in spite of the fact that Cromwell, who was sitting on the next bench, turned to him angrily and said, 'What ails thee? Art thou mad? Canst thou not sit still and be quiet?' As a result the president ruled that the court would adjourn to consider Charles's proposal. In the small room of the Court of Wards to which they adjourned, Cromwell brought all the force of his personality to bear upon Downes and some other waverers, calling Charles 'the hardest-hearted man upon the earth', and insisting that the court proceed to sentence him. After half-an-hour's argument he had his way, and the court re-assembled. Bradshaw made a polished and learned speech asserting that the King was subject to law and that law was made by Parliament and by the people. 'The King is but an officer in trust', and Charles had broken his trust by seeking to uproot Parliament,

'The hardest-hearted man upon the earth'

183

The death warrant of Charles I, which stated that
the King 'be put to death by the severing of his
head from his body'. Fifty-nine people signed the
warrant; the first signature is that of John
Bradshaw, and the third, of Oliver Cromwell.

...for the tryinge and adiudginge of Charles
...England, Januarÿ xxix Anno Dni 1648.

...standeth convicted attaynted and condemned ...
...was pronounced against him ... to be put to death ...
...not remayneth to be done, Theise are therefore ...
...open streete before ... the ...
...of ... in the ... and ... in the afternoone ...
...this warrant And theise ... Officers ...
...assistinge vnto you in this service ...

the great bulwark of the liberties of the people of England. 'There is a contract and a bargain made between the King and his people, and your oath is taken: and certainly, Sir, the bond is reciprocal.' Charles had broken the contract and made war on his subjects. With real passion Bradshaw declared, 'Sir, the charge hath called you a Tyrant, a Traitor, a Murderer, and a public enemy to the Commonwealth of England. Sir, it had been well if that any of all these terms might rightly and justly have been spared.'

Charles attempted to speak in his own defence, but Bradshaw protested that it was too late for him to do so. 'You have not owned us as a court, and you look upon us as a sort of people met together: and we know what language we received from your party.' He insisted on continuing his speech, which ended with the sentence of death. Charles again sought to speak, but the president declared that a prisoner was never heard after sentence had been pronounced. As Charles still tried to speak he was hustled away by the soldiers. His last words were – 'I am not suffered for to speak. Expect what justice other people will have.'

The King spent his last days mainly in prayer and religious meditation with Bishop Juxon. On the day of the execution, 30 January 1649, he put on an extra shirt so that he would not, when undressed on the scaffold, shiver from cold and give the impression of fear. The weather was icy. He was taken from St James's in the morning and was kept waiting for several hours in Whitehall, the royal palace where so many of the happiest hours of his life had been spent. He had not returned to it since leaving seven years ago, after the disastrous attempt to arrest the five members. In the interval the palace had been used by the Parliament and then by the army, and was now in a sorry state of dilapidation. The scaffold had been erected in front of Inigo Jones's beautiful Banqueting House, one of the few parts of the palace of Charles's time to survive to our own day. It was sadly fallen from its former splendour with most of the windows blocked up. The magnificent ceiling painted by Rubens, which the King had loved so much that he had refused to permit the presentation of a masque in the room for fear that smoke from the candles would damage it, was, however, untouched. The King walked through the room and out onto the scaffold, through one of the windows. Troopers on horseback surrounded the scaffold so that the crowds were kept well back. Charles realised that he could not hope to be heard by the public, but there were shorthand writers on the scaffold. His last speech was to be accurately recorded, and rapidly disseminated in pamphlets and news-sheets. He had prepared some notes for his speech which he brought out and used. He began:

> I never did begin the war with the two Houses of Parliament, and I call on God to witness (to whom I must shortly make an account) that I never did intend to incroach upon their privileges. They began upon me. It is the militia they began upon, they confest that the Militia was mine, but they thought it fit to have it from me. And to be short, if anybody will look but to the dates of the commissions, their commissions and mine, and likewise to their declarations, will see clearly that they began these unhappy troubles, not I.

But although he declared that he was innocent of causing the war, he knew that as a Christian he had sinned, and that God was punishing him. Referring to his agreement to Strafford's death, he said, 'An unjust sentence that I suffered to take effect, is punished now by an unjust sentence upon me.' He forgave his opponents for what they had done, and laid down his political testament that a national synod, 'freely called, freely debating among themselves' should settle the religious question. About temporal politics, he said,

> As for the King, the laws of the Land will clearly instruct you for that, therefore . . . I only give you a touch of it. For the People, and truly I desire their liberty and freedom, as much as anybody whomsoever, but I must tell you, that their liberty and freedom consist in having of government, those laws by which their life and their goods may be most their own. It is not for having a share in government, Sirs: that is nothing pertaining to them. A subject and a sovereign are clean different things. . . .

'A subject and a sovereign are clean different things'

It was for this right of his people to be governed according to the old laws, and not subject to the arbitrary power of the sword, that he had contended, and for this he was dying, 'and therefore I tell you . . . that I am the Martyr of the people'. Reminded by the Bishop of London of the need to make it quite clear that he was not a Catholic, he declared that he died 'a Christian according to the profession of the Church of England

RIGHT The palace at
Whitehall outside which
the King met his death.
The palace had been the
King's principal residence,
but had stood half-empty
for the last seven years of
his reign, used by
Parliament and later
occupied by the army.

OPPOSITE The beautiful
Banqueting House,
designed by Inigo Jones
(with a ceiling painted by
Rubens), through which
Charles walked to the
scaffold. The windows
were now boarded up and
the room dark and bare.

as I found it left me by my father'. Then he was prepared for the
execution, taking off his jewels, his cloak and his doublet, and
arranging his hair under a cap to keep it out of the way of the
axe. At the King's sign that he was ready, the executioner
raised the axe and severed the head at one blow. A great groan
went up from the crowd, which was immediately cleared from
the street by the troopers.

Charles's execution completed the work of his trial in blotting
out for everyone except the most convinced of his political
opponents, all the mistakes of his earlier career. The dignity and
nobility with which he confronted death were impressive.
Even Andrew Marvell, the Puritan poet, in the course of his
panegyric in honour of the King's great adversary, *An Horatian
Ode for Cromwell's Return from Ireland*, had the breadth of

A Noble Death

The king met his death with the same dignity with which he had faced his trial. The sympathy of the crowd was with the King, and when the axe fell, a spectator recorded 'there was such a groan by the thousands then present as I never heard before, and I desire I may never hear again'.

RIGHT One of the two shirts which Charles wore at his execution. It was a bitterly cold morning, and the King wore two shirts so that he would not shiver on the scaffold and seem to be afraid.
BELOW Bishop Juxon, with whom Charles spent the last few days before his death in prayer and meditation.

OPPOSITE Title page of *The Confessions of Richard Brandon* showing the execution of the King; Brandon was the King's executioner and the City's principal hangman.
BELOW The Juxon Medal, given by Charles to the Bishop on the scaffold.

THE
CONFESSION

June 25 OF *1649*

Richard Brandon

The Hangman (upon his Death-bed) concerning His beheading his late Majesty, C H A R L E S the first, King of Great Brittain; and his Proteſtation and Vow touching the ſame; the manner how he was terrified in Conſcience; the Apparitions and Viſions which apeared unto him; the great judgment that befell him three dayes before he dy'd ; and the manner how he was carryed to White-Chappell Church-yard on Thurſday night laſt, the ſtrange Actions that happened thereupon; With the merry conceits of the Crowne Cook, and his providing mourning Cords for the Buriall.

Printed in the year Year, of the Hang-mans down-fall, 1649.

RIGHT Andrew Marvell. Although he was a follower of Cromwell, he was sufficiently moved by Charles's death to record it in sympathetic verse.

OPPOSITE Title page of John Milton's *Tenure of Kings and Magistrates* published on 13 February 1649. Milton was an ardent Puritan and supporter of Cromwell; his pamphlet defended the theory of popular sovereignty in answer to Royalist propaganda which was rife after the death of the King.

sympathy to pen the famous lines on Charles's conduct on that day:

> He nothing common did, or mean,
> Upon that memorable scene:
> But, with his keener eye
> The Axe's edge did try:
>
> Nor call'd the Gods with vulgar spite
> To vindicate his helpless Right
> But bow'd his comely head
> Down, as upon a bed.

The legend of the Martyr King was much enhanced by the publication, in defiance of the censorship, of *Eikon Basilike, The Pourtraicture of his Sacred Majestie in his Solitudes and Sufferings*. The book contained prayers, religious reflections and

192

{ Ex dono Authoris Feb. 1648 }

THE TENURE OF KINGS AND MAGISTRATES:

PROVING,

That it is Lawfull, and hath been held so through all Ages, for any, who have the Power, to call to account a Tyrant, or wicked KING, and after due conviction, to depose, and put him to death; if the ordinary MAGISTRATE have neglected, or deny'd to doe it.

And that they, who of late, so much blame Deposing, are the Men that did it themselves.

The Author, J. M.(ilton)

Miltons Tenure of Kings

LONDON,

Printed by *Matthew Simmons*, at the Gilded Lyon in Aldersgate Street, 1649.

Imaginary reconstruction
of the execution of
Charles I, by Weesop.

Portrait of Cromwell from
the Roll of Acounts for
Ireland for the years
1649–56. Two months
after the death of Charles,
Cromwell set out for
Ireland to crush the
rebelling Catholics.

Guil: Marshall delinea: et Sculpsit.

The Explanation of the EMBLEME.

Ponderibus *genus omne mali, probris, gravatus,*
Vtq, ferenda ferens, Palma ut Depressa, resurgo.

Though clogg'd with weights of miseries
Palm-like Depress'd, I higher rise.

Ac, velut undarum Fluctûs Ventiq, furorem
Grati Populi Rupes immota repello.
Clarior è tenebris, cœlestis stella, corusco.
Victor et æternùm-felici pace triumpho.

And as th'unmoved Rock out-brave's
The boistrous Windes and rageing waves
So triumph I. And shine more bright
In sad Affliction's Darksom night.

Auro Fulgentem rutilo gemmisq, micantem,
At curis Gravidam spernendo calco Coronam.

That Splendid, but yet toilsom Crown
Regardlesly I trample down.

Spinosam, at ferri facilem, quo Spes mea,Christi
Auxilio, Nobis non est tractare molestum.

With joie I take this Crown of thorn,
Though sharp, yet easie to be born.

Æternam, fixis fidei, semperq,-beatam
In Cœlos oculis Specto, Nobisq, paratam.

That heav'nlie Crown, already mine,
I View with eies of Faith divine.

Quod Vanum est, sperno; quod Christi Gratia præbet
Amplecti studium est: Virtutis Gloria merces.

I slight vain things; and do embrace
Glorie, the just reward of Grace.

Τὸ Χῖ ȣ̇δὲν ἠδίκησε τὼ πόλιν, ȣ̇δὲ τὸ Κάππα.

G. D.

judgments on the history of his reign, and was supposed to be printed from papers left behind by the King himself. Its principal author was a clergyman named John Gauden, later promoted to a bishopric as his reward, but he had used documents given to him in the autumn of 1648 by Charles himself. It provided an accurate picture of how Charles wanted to be presented to the world. He admitted that he was a man who had made mistakes, and had committed sins. This was a chastened statement of the theory of Divine Right, compared with the grandiose claims put forward by his father in *The True Law of Free Monarchies*. But he did not depart from the essentials of his political and religious faith. The King was answerable to God alone and not to his subjects, and his primordial responsibility was to preserve the true doctrine of the Christian religion, represented by the Church of England. For that Charles was prepared to die, as he had demonstrated. The book had a great success, and was only a part of a great mass of legend that began to grow around the King and his execution. The obvious comparison with the execution of Christ was frequently made, and Charles was represented, as in the frontispiece of *Eikon Basilike*, with a crown of thorns illuminated by a heavenly radiance. Nevertheless, for all the popularity of this celebration of the royal martyr in words and pictures, there was no effective Royalist movement in England. Cromwell and the army leaders had correctly calculated that the removal of the King would clear the ground for a political settlement.

OPPOSITE Frontispiece of *Eikon Basilike*, published on the day of the King's burial. The book was accepted by the Royalists as the King's authentic record of his sufferings and religious meditations and it sold in great numbers, reprinting thirty times within the year.

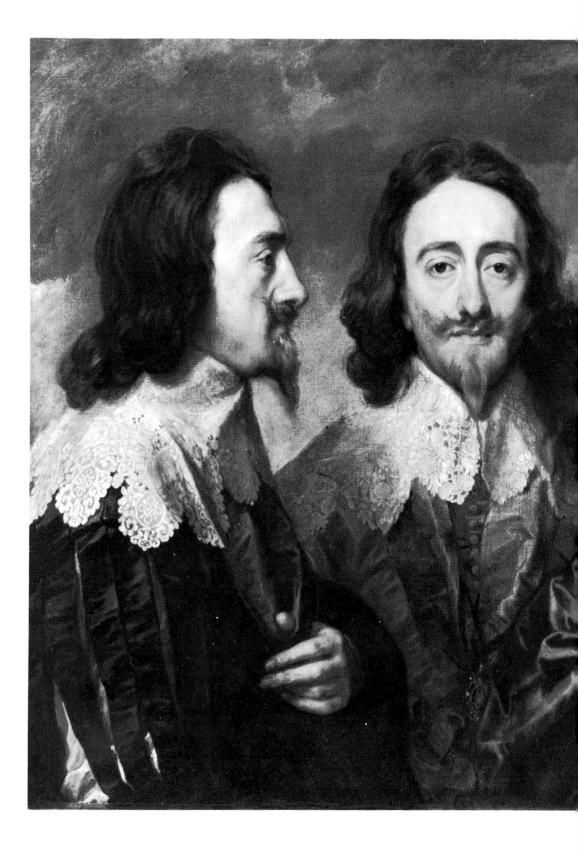

8
Charles I:
Tyrant
or Martyr?
1625-49

'MEN WONDERED', wrote Lucy Hutchinson, the wife of a Puritan colonel, 'that so good a man should be so bad a King.' The contrast is indeed striking between Charles's virtues as a private man, and his political failure. One of the most attractive features of his character was expressed in his deep love for Henrietta Maria and can be seen in the letters he wrote to her during their separation in and after the war. These letters are far removed in tone and style from the stilted formality that the Parliamentarians ascribed to them, when they published forgeries of the royal correspondence for propaganda purposes. 'Dear heart' or 'Sweetheart', Charles calls his wife, and ends invariably 'Eternally thine'. He frequently assures her that only the thought of her love gives him the strength to continue the struggle with his opponents. Written in direct and straightforward language, they are bound to awaken sympathy for Charles in the reader.

His personal charm is also attested by the favourable impression he made on those who knew him during his years of captivity. Sir Philip Warwick, for a time the King's secretary, contrasted the formalities on which Charles insisted, as the due of a King, with his modesty and politeness as a man. He wrote in a brief sketch of Charles's character:

> His deportment was very majestic, for he could not let fall his dignity ... for though he was far from pride, yet he was careful of majesty, and would be approached with respect and reverence. ... His way of urging was very civil and patient, for he seldom contradicted another by his authority, but by reason ... he offered his exception by this civil introduction. By your favour, Sir, I think otherwise on this or that ground.

In the first years of the reign Charles had made his Court one of the most formal in Europe. Only Henrietta Maria herself could be seated in the royal presence; the King dined in state, with great ceremonial, and in public. Charles insisted on this ceremony, not because he personally enjoyed pomp and the marking out of his royal eminence, but as way of underlining a political principle. Life at Charles's Court, although full of ceremonial, was not unduly luxurious. The great feasts and banquets of his father's day were replaced by more aesthetic entertainments, the plays and masques, with music and dancing, in which both King and Queen delighted. Charles was himself

PREVIOUS PAGES Charles I in three positions, painted by Van Dyck in 1637 and sent to Rome to help Bernini execute a bust of the King. When Bernini saw the painting, he said: 'Never have I seen a countenance more unfortunate.'

abstemious in his diet. Warwick tells us that 'he seldom ate of above three dishes at most, nor drank above thrice, a glass of small beer, another of claret wine, and the last of water'. As a result, in contrast to the physical debility of his father who was old before his time, he remained in good health through all the stresses and exertions of the war and his subsequent imprisonment.

Charles has been called 'intellectual without being intelligent', and this may be accepted, at least as far as concerns his lack of intelligence in political matters. He was not especially bookish. Warwick reported that 'his proportion of books was but small, having learnt more by the ear than by study'. Nevertheless he does seem to have liked literature, and to have read a considerable amount. In his captivity he read the Italian poets Ariosto and Tasso in English translation, Spenser's *Faerie Queen*, Shakespeare's plays, and the Anglican theologians Hooker, Lancelot Andrewes and Laud. At the time of his death he had in his possession a French romance, *Cassandre*, by Gautier de la Calprenède. His love of art and music are well known, and his good taste in art is attested by the large number of really good pieces that he assembled in the royal collection. He enjoyed hunting, like all gentlemen of his day. Charles was, in short, a serious-minded and cultivated English gentleman of his generation.

He was devoutly religious throughout his life, insisting on attendance at daily prayers whatever the circumstances. During the period of personal rule, he took a detailed interest in Laud's attempt to reform the Church. In his last years he read the Bible every day, noting his reflections in the margin. At the time of his visit to Spain, he is said to have surprised the Catholic priests who were sent to argue with him about religion, by the extent of his theological knowledge. The events of his life reinforced this knowledge, as theological and political problems became steadily more intertwined.

His opponents have sometimes said that his religion was subordinate to his political creed, that he opposed Presbyterianism because it taught rebellion, and advocated Anglo-Catholicism because it reinforced royal authority. He certainly did hold those beliefs, but it would be a misreading of his character and of the climate of thought in the mid-seventeenth century to think that

'An intellectual without being intelligent'

201

The Royal Patron

Charles I was not an extravagant man and his Court was not lavish by contemporary standards. But he had a genuine appreciation of art and he spent a great deal as a patron of the arts, both collecting great works and supporting living artists such as Van Dyck and Rubens. His magnificent collection of paintings was dispersed during the Interregnum.

BELOW *The Vase Bearers,* one of nine panels by Mantegna celebrating the Triumph of Caesar which Charles purchased. Among the other masters whose paintings Charles collected were Titian, Raphael, Tintoretto, Correggio and Giorgione.

ABOVE *Peace and War* by
Rubens. The painting, an
allegory of European
peace and felicity, was
presented to Charles by
Rubens when he came to
England in 1629 as
ambassador from
Philip IV of Spain.
According to Rubens, he
'soon happily established
a basis of peace between
those princes'.

RIGHT Van Dyck's
*Self-portrait with a
Sunflower*. Van Dyck
worked in England for the
last nine years of his life,
from 1632 to 1641. He had
immense prestige and
enormous practice at
Charles's Court.

PROIICIO AMPVLL.

Charles was interested in science as well as the arts, and among those to whom he gave his patronage were William Harvey (*right*) who discovered the circulation of the blood, and Sir Theodore Turquet de Mayerne (*above*), the physician to James I and Charles, who first established in England the clinical study of medicine.

46

ESQ. PACISCOR IN AVRO .

ABOVE A travelling quack; medical knowledge was at a very early stage, and for most people the only hope of relief from pain and sickness was from such charlatans.

political concerns were uppermost in his mind. Very few, certainly not the King, thought that religion and politics could be separated. He did condemn Presbyterianism, and the Covenant, because of their political implications because 'this damned covenant is the child of rebellion, and breathes nothing but treason'. But he condemned them also on more fundamental religious grounds. By abandoning bishops the Presbyterians had broken the apostolic succession that linked Christians of his day with the first disciples of Christ. He explained to Henrietta Maria that no member of the Church of England

> . . . can with a safe conscience so far communicate with any of the Calvinists as to receive the sacrament of the Eucharist, there being none of the reformed churches abroad (except the Lutherans) that can justify the succession of their priests, which if this [the Church of England] could not undoubtedly do, she should have one son less for me.

Thus, although he was firm in his rejection of Roman Catholicism, there was a sense in which his Puritan critics were correct in thinking that he abhorred Presbyterianism more than Popery. Although he believed that their Church had been corrupted and needed reformation, Roman Catholics were in his eyes members of a true Church, whereas Presbyterians were not. He respected his wife's religion, and never sought to convert her to his own. He had promised this when they married and he kept his promise, in spite of the political difficulties caused him by the Queen's religion. When Henrietta Maria pleaded with him to accept Presbyterianism for political reasons, he replied: 'Make the case thine own. With what patience would'est thou give ear to him who should persuade thee, for worldly respects, to leave the communion of the Roman Church.'

But all Charles's virtues as a husband, a father, and a private individual, should not blind us to the shortcomings of his political conduct. His failure as a politician appeared first of all in the shyness, taciturnity and reserve which often made a bad impression on those with whom he was brought into contact by public business. He seemed cold and ungrateful even to those who served him well. Bishop Burnet recorded that the Earl of Lothian, who had lived at Charles's Court in the early years of his reign, said that:

His temper was sullen, even to a moroseness. This led him to a grave, reserved deportment, in which he forgot the civilities and the affability that the nation naturally loved, to which they had been long accustomed: nor did he, in his outward deportment, take any pains to oblige any person whatsoever, so far from that, he had such an ungracious way of shewing favour that the manner of bestowing it was almost as mortifying as the favour was obliging.

This is, no doubt, an extreme statement, and the words 'sullen' and 'morose' do not have quite their modern sense. But there was a melancholy air to Charles which comes out in all his portraits. The sculptor Bernini said in 1637 when he saw Van Dyck's portrait of Charles in three positions, 'Never have I beheld a countenance more unfortunate.'

There can be no doubt that Charles was often tactless not only in his dealings with individuals, but more seriously, in his speeches to Parliament, as when he told them that he was not threatening them since 'he scorned to threaten any but his equals'. This was a view expressed again and again in different words in his speeches to various Parliaments on occasions when he obviously was threatening them. He would have been wiser to have refrained from underlining it in such a way. Lack of tact might seem to be a minor defect, but it points to a major reason for Charles's political failure. To be tactless may mean that one is unable to see how one's words and manner will appear to other people, to be unable to see things from their point of view. This lack of imagination, this inflexibility of mind, was the greatest of the King's political failings. It meant that during the non-Parliamentary period of his reign he got far out of touch with the opinions of the majority of the politically-conscious nation. As a result there developed the political crisis that was to produce the Civil War.

His lack of awareness of the other point of view was another side of Charles's legalistic way of thinking. His entire reign was filled with appeals to the letter of the law which disregarded the political realities of the situation. He began in this way during his conflict with his first Parliaments, when the Venetian ambassador reported that 'with the key of the laws he seeks to open the door to absolute power', and he continued during the period of personal rule, which has been called an orgy of antiquarianism. If his lawyers could dig up a medieval precedent,

PREVIOUS PAGES Charles I dining in public at Whitehall Palace, by Houckgeest. Charles frequently ate in public, not because he enjoyed the pomp and ceremony, but as a way of asserting his position as King.

Charles thought that his case was won. So it was in the short term. But resentments built up that were rapidly to take the Long Parliament beyond the restoration of ancient rights, into an attempt to alter the balance of the constitution. They did so largely because of distrust of the King, which forced them to take extreme measures restricting royal authority, far more drastic in practice than could be justified in theory. Charles never considered submitting permanently to this legal revolution. He claimed later that he had been 'couzen'd' into the fatal step of signing the bill that took away his right to dissolve the Long Parliament without its own consent: 'I was surprised with it instantly after I made that base sinful concession, concerning the earl of Strafford.' He made concessions to his opponents, but only in the spirit of bowing before the storm, hoping to recover his full prerogative, by whatever means, in the future. Typical of his mode of reasoning was the justification which he gave to Henrietta Maria, when he sought to explain, on 30 November 1646, why he had agreed to the establishment of Presbyterianism for three years: 'I never heard that any right was yielded as long as the claim was kept up, which is done clearly in this case by having a debate of divines how the Church shall be governed.'

' That base sinful concession, concerning the earl of Strafford'

On this occasion, as on many others from the beginning of his reign to the end, Charles exposed himself to accusations of duplicity and prevarication, if not downright dishonesty. He himself could never see this. He prided himself on having a clear conscience and he frequently offered his word of honour as a king. Yet, on many occasions, he pursued secret plots and intrigues, promising quite different and incompatible things to different people. This was so in 1641, and again in 1646 and 1647 when he was trying desperately to organise intervention from Ireland or the Continent at the same time as he negotiated with the Scots and with the English Parliamentarians. Already in 1628, when the opposition in the Commons had refused to accept his word as a sufficient guarantee of the Petition of Right, it had been clear that many people did not trust him. Lack of belief in his trustworthiness increased steadily, until Cromwell and Ireton decided that the only solution was to remove him from the political stage. A politician may be well advised to contemplate alternative courses of action, but one in Charles's

209

position could not afford to play so devious a game. In any case his intrigues always proved futile.

The psychological process by which Charles convinced himself that he was being perfectly honest is a well-known one, and one which we all share to some degree. We all tend to place that interpretation on a complex series of propositions, which best fits our own way of thinking, and usually, therefore, our own interests. In the confused and self-contradictory jungles of English constitutional law and of Biblical exegesis, there was immense scope for casuistry. Charles carried belief in his own righteousness to an extreme. He could always justify his actions to himself, and he could not see how they seemed to be dishonest to other people, putting such accusations down to malicious and self-interested cavilling. The end result was that true statesmanship completely escaped his grasp. He faced a difficult situation, but it was his failure of statesmanship that produced the tragedy of the Civil War. From 1640 onwards he remained blind to the need for compromise. He made concessions, but showed that he intended to repudiate them if he possibly could. As this was so obvious, they could not be used as the basis for a settlement, and his opponents were forced to make ever greater demands to guard themselves against a royal *coup* exposing them to the penalties for treason. A process of escalation began that ended in the Civil War.

He can, in a way, be said to have been looking for a martyr's crown long before the regicides gave him one. For he did not pursue a determined and energetic policy of resistance. As Bishop Burnet put it, 'he minded little things too much, and was more concerned in the drawing of a paper than in fighting a battle'. Although he was rigid and obstinate he was not at all confident in his own judgment, and thus often vacillated between different lines of action. He was shattered by his experiences in May 1641, when the hysteria of the London mob and the calculating pressure of the Parliamentary leaders forced him to sacrifice Strafford. Deprived of Strafford's confident advice, he never again found an adviser on whom he could totally rely. Often he seemed to sink into a sort of apathy, and be unable to make up his mind to any course of action. The final months of the war, from the battle of Naseby to his escape from Oxford, were one such period. His letters to Henrietta Maria in

210

212

1646 reveal his unhappiness at having to make decisions without any advisers on whom he could rely. He wrote:

> There was never a man so alone as I, and therefore very much to be excused for the committing of any errour, because I have reason to suspect everything that these advised me, and to distrust mine own single opinion, having no living soul to help me.

Clarendon wrote in his *History of The Great Rebellion,* that:

> He had an excellent understanding but was not confident enough of it: which made him oftentimes change his own opinion for a worse, and follow the advice of men that did not judge so well as himself. This made him more irresolute than the conjecture of his affairs would admit; if he had been of a rougher and more imperious nature he would have found more respect and duty.

Clarendon who, as Edward Hyde, was one of those who rallied to the King in the autumn of 1641 and was close to him for the next few months, brings forward no examples of Charles's correct judgments; in the last resort, if the King decided to follow bad advice it was a sign of his own bad judgment. Nor was it the case that he could have obtained obedience 'if he had been of a rougher and more imperious nature'. The trouble with Charles's policy was not that he gave way too easily, but that he refused to give way when it was necessary that he should, that he gave way too late and with such a bad grace that he lost the initiative to his opponents. Bishop Burnet's assessment is sounder than Clarendon's. He wrote that:

> His reign both in peace and war was a continual series of errors: so that it does not appear that he had a true judgement of things. He was out of measure set on following his humour, but unreasonably feeble to those whom he trusted, chiefly the Queen.

Most nineteenth-century historians were very hostile to Charles, calling him a tyrant. When the battle for Parliamentary liberty was still fresh in men's minds, a balanced detachment was not to be expected. Macaulay said that he detested Charles I, and the Whig version of his reign was confirmed by S.R. Gardiner in his multi-volumed *History of the Civil War,* which is still the definitive work for the narrative history of the period. Gardiner, with his measured tones and academic caution, in the end condemns Charles as roundly as Macaulay had done. In recent years a more charitable view has been taken, and most twentieth-century biographies of Charles I are of the nature of

OPPOSITE Edward Hyde, Earl of Clarendon. An early critic of Charles I in Parliament, he became Charles's chief civilian adviser during the Civil War and he was the main architect of the Restoration settlement in 1660. His *History of the Great Rebellion* was written mainly in exile between 1667 and his death in 1674, when he had fallen out of favour with Charles II.

hagiographies. His virtues are praised, and his faults are for-gotten, except that he is depicted as not being ruthless enough to deal with his wicked opponents. Even academic studies which do not go to these lengths, tend to be much more sympathetic to Charles than those who wrote in the nineteenth-century Whig tradition.

One can see why this is so. For one reason, the modern world has seen totalitarian dictators whose exploits make Charles's 'tyranny' seem mild indeed. Another factor is a more critical attitude towards the Parliamentary monarchy that was sought by Charles's opponents and which was finally achieved in 1689. In the sub-Marxist interpretations which spread through his-torical studies under the influence of R.H. Tawney, Charles's reign was seen in terms of a conflict between feudalism and capitalism. According to this version the Parliamentarians were sordid capitalists who disguised their rapacious designs under the cloak of liberty, while Charles and his ministers were the defenders of an old feudal order that took more care of the interests of the poor. A few scraps of evidence from the pro-ceedings of the prerogative courts in the period of personal government have been greatly overstretched to maintain this interpretation. In reality it is romantic nonsense to think that absolutism would lead to better treatment of the poor. That was not the way it seemed at the time, nor does sober modern research support that view. In the seventeenth century money stuck to the hands of those who handled it on behalf of the King. State intervention was usually an operation designed to be profitable for the King himself and for his servants. The condi-tion of the poor was far worse under the absolute monarchy of France, where taxes were collected by force of arms, than in Britain, dominated by the gentry and rapidly becoming a liberal, semi-capitalist society.

The importance of the reign of Charles I was that, during it, England did not become an absolute monarchy on the Conti-nental pattern. This was largely the result of developments in England that derived from the distant past, of the social and economic structure, of political institutions, and of geographical facts. Attempts to stress the similarities between England and the major monarchical states of Western Europe in the early seventeenth century are not convincing. Nevertheless the play

A puritan satire on the defeat of the King's party. The ark, representing the
Commonwealth and Assembly of Divines, contains the House of Lords,
without King or judges, the House of Commons and the Assembly.
Floundering in the water are Charles I, Henrietta Maria, Laud, Strafford,
Prince Rupert and other Royalists. The medallion portraits represent the
army leaders.

of personalities and the development of political conflict in Charles's reign were also factors. It was conceivable that Parliament might have atrophied, as representative bodies did in most Continental countries at this time. A verdict in favour of Charles is a verdict in favour of traditional absolute government. This was by no means the same thing as modern dictatorship. Charles sincerely believed it, when he said that he wanted the liberty of the subject as much as any man. But, as he went on to say, the liberty of the subject did not mean the right to a share in the government. It meant the right to possess one's property in tranquillity, and to live peaceably under the control and guidance of a social hierarchy, at the peak of which was the King, responsible not to his subjects but to God alone. Theorists of absolute royal power on the Continent said the same thing, declaring that an absolute monarch was not a despot, freed from all legal rules. Royal absolutism provided negative liberty, in which the traditional rights of individuals, groups, communities, and provinces, were by and large respected. But it could not provide a positive liberty, a system under which the political will of the nation was expressed by representative institutions that had a share in decision-making. The growth of such a system by which the conflicts of a more complex society could be moderated and compromised, demanded the victory of Parliament over Charles I. Political liberty in the modern sense could only come through the destruction of the royal power that Charles believed that he had inherited as a trust to be passed on intact to his heir.

Supporters of the King, from contemporaries like Warwick and Clarendon to some modern writers, have argued that Charles's interpretation of the royal prerogative was the 'correct' and legal one, and that Parliament faced him with a revolutionary challenge. Opponents of the King, from the seventeenth century to the nineteenth, took the opposite line and argued that Charles was attempting to overturn a previously established balance of power between Crown and Parliament. Surely the truth lies somewhere in between. The system of government of the early seventeenth century could have evolved in either direction and both sides could cite precedents. It could have evolved towards a stronger monarchy, or, as it actually did, towards a Parliamentary, limited and constitutional monarchy. Legally it is probably true that Charles was acting more in the spirit of previous precedent than were his opponents, and it does not seem fair to call him a tyrant. But the question that had to be fought out in the Civil War was the question of which way the system would develop. It could not stay in suspended animation, in the deadlocked position produced by the conflict between King and Parliament in 1629. As emerged with the Scottish troubles, a relatively small problem was sufficient to call in question everything Charles thought he had achieved in his years without Parliament.

The crisis forced both sides to adopt more extreme positions. If Charles had won the war there could hardly have been a return to the *status quo*. There must have been the development of stronger monarchical power, as happened in other European states at this time. Because he lost the war, the Parliamentary claim triumphed. This did not appear to be so in 1649, or at any time before the restoration of the monarchy in 1660, but it was so all the same. Charles ii was restored on conditions, because he accepted what his father had refused. It was symbolic that one of his first political acts after his father's execution was to sign the Covenant, which his father had refused to do. In the short run, because of the war and the religious, political and social ferment it produced, Parliament seemed to have been defeated almost as much as the King, a point which Charles made to good effect at his trial. One reason for this eclipse of Parliament was the fact that Charles refused to play the part of a limited monarch, on the terms offered in 1646 and 1647. He could have been restored to the throne on such terms at any time before the outbreak of the Second Civil War in 1648. As much as any man, Charles was responsible for the fact that England experimented with republican constitutions for a few years, before his son was restored to the throne as a limited monarch. By showing that he would not whole-heartedly accept such a role Charles condemned himself to death.

HOUSE OF STUART

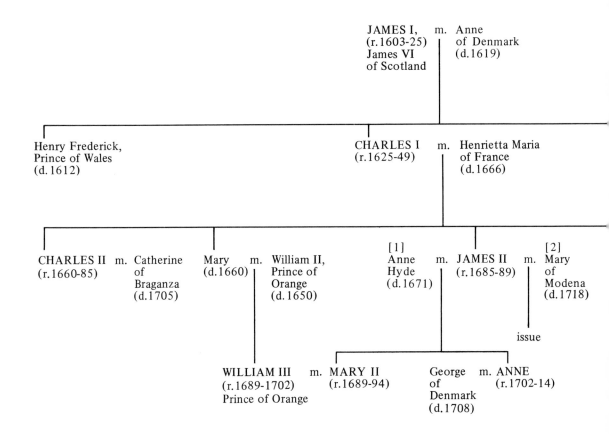

JAMES I,   m.   Anne
(r.1603-25)   of Denmark
James VI   (d.1619)
of Scotland

Henry Frederick,   CHARLES I   m.   Henrietta Maria
Prince of Wales   (r.1625-49)   of France
(d.1612)   (d.1666)

CHARLES II m. Catherine   Mary   m.   William II,   [1]   [2]
(r.1660-85)   of   (d.1660)   Prince of   Anne   m.   JAMES II   m.   Mary
             Braganza   Orange   Hyde   (r.1685-89)   of
             (d.1705)   (d.1650)   (d.1671)   Modena
                                                                    (d.1718)

                                                                                        issue

                                WILLIAM III   m.   MARY II   George   m. ANNE
                                (r.1689-1702)   (r.1689-94)   of   (r.1702-14)
                                Prince of Orange   Denmark
                                                         (d.1708)

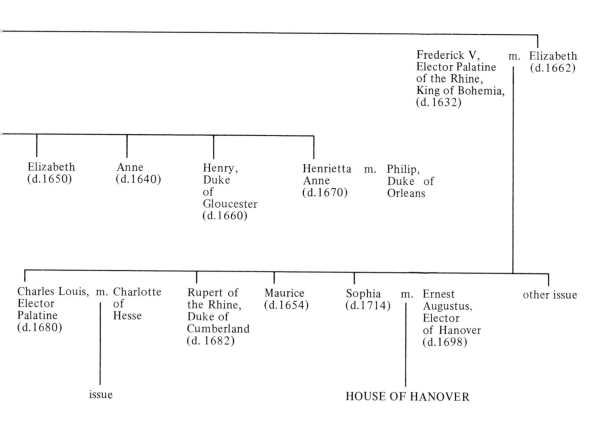

Frederick V,
Elector Palatine
of the Rhine,
King of Bohemia,
(d. 1632)   m.   Elizabeth
(d.1662)

Elizabeth
(d.1650)

Anne
(d.1640)

Henry,
Duke
of
Gloucester
(d.1660)

Henrietta   m.   Philip,
Anne   Duke of
(d.1670)   Orleans

Charles Louis,   m.   Charlotte
Elector   of
Palatine   Hesse
(d.1680)

issue

Rupert of
the Rhine,
Duke of
Cumberland
(d. 1682)

Maurice
(d.1654)

Sophia   m.   Ernest
(d.1714)   Augustus,
                    Elector
                    of Hanover
                    (d.1698)

HOUSE OF HANOVER

other issue

Select bibliography

G. P. V. Akrigg, *Jacobean Pageant or the Court of King James I*, 1962

E. Almack, ed., *Eikon Basilike, or the King's Book*, 1907

M. Ashley, *Life in Stuart England*, 1964

R. Ashton, 'Charles I and the City' in *Essays in the Economic and Social History of Tudor and Stuart England*, ed. F. J. Fisher, 1961

J. P. Cooper, 'Differences between English and continental government in the early 17th Century' in *Britain and the Netherlands*, eds., J. S. Bromley and E. H. Kossman, 1960

S. R. Gardiner, *The First Two Stuarts and The Puritan Revolution, 1876*, new paperback edition, 1970

J. H. Hexter, *The reign of King Pym*, 1941

C. Hibbert, *Charles I*, 1968

H. Hulme, 'Charles I and the constitution' in *Conflict in Stuart England*, eds. W. A. Aiken and B. D. Henning, 1960

E. Hyde, Earl of Clarendon, *Selections from*, ed. G. Huehns, 1955

E. W. Ives, *The English Revolution 1600–1660*, 1968

H. F. Kearney, *The eleven years' tyranny of Charles I*, 1962

J. P. Kenyon, *The Stuarts*, 1958

R. Lockyer, ed., *The Trial of Charles I*, 1959

C. Oman, *Henrietta Maria*, 1936

Sir Charles Petrie, ed., *The Letters, Speeches and Proclamations of Charles I*, new ed. 1968

I. Roots, *The Great Rebellion 1642–1660*, 1966

J. R. Tanner, *English Constitutional Conflicts of the Seventeenth Century, 1603–1689*, 1928, paperback ed. 1962

H. R. Trevor-Roper, *Archbishop Laud, 1573–1645*, 1940
The Trial and Execution of King Charles I, Scholar Press 1966 (a facsimile reproduction of contemporary official accounts)

C. V. Wedgwood, *The King's Peace, 1637–1641*, 1955, paperback ed. 1966; *The King's War 1641–1647*, 1958, paperback ed. 1966; *The Trial of Charles I*, 1964, paperback ed. 1967; *Thomas Wentworth, First Earl of Strafford, 1593–1641, a revaluation*, 1961

E. C. Williams, *Anne of Denmark*, 1970

E. Wingfield-Stratford, *Charles, King of England, 1600–1637*, 1949; *King Charles and King Pym*, 1949; *King Charles the Martyr*, 1950

A. H. Woolrych, *Battles of the English Civil War*, 1961

Index